My Heart's at Home

0-8054-1658-7

Published by Broadman & Holman Publishers, Nashville, Tennessee
Acquisitions and Development Editor: Leonard G. Goss
Page Composition: Leslie Joslin, Gray, Tennessee

Dewey Decimal Classification: 248
Subject Heading: PARENTING/WORKING MOTHERS
Library of Congress Card Catalog number: 98-31336

Unless otherwise stated, all Scripture quotations are from the Holy Bible,
New International Version, © copyright 1973, 1978, 1984.
Other versions are marked NASB, the New American Standard Bible,
© Copyright The Lockman Foundation, 1960, 1962, 1963, 1968,
1971, 1972, 1973, 1975, 1977, 1995;
NKJV, New King James Version, copyright © 1979, 1980, 1982,
Thomas Nelson, Inc., Publishers.

Library of Congress Cataloging-in-Publication Data
Larmoyeux, Mary, 1951
     My heart's at home : encouragement for working moms / Mary
Larmoyeux.
     p.   cm
     ISBN 0-8054-1658-7
     1. Working mothers--Religious Life.. 2. Child rearing--Religious
aspects--Christianity. I. Title II. Title: My heart is at home.
BV4529.L26   1999
248.8'431--dc21
                      98-31336
                      CIP

1 2 3 4 5 03 02 01 00 99

To my mother,
Lucile Miller May.

Mom, thank you for loving Dad for fifty-one years.
Your life with him proclaimed faithfulness and commitment.
When Dad died he was remembered as a man of integrity who loved his wife.
What a legacy you and he have given me!

And Mom, thank you for modeling unselfishness.
You put the needs of your husband and children ahead of your own desires.
You recognized the high calling of a mother and made countless sacrifices while raising
Nancy, Lawrence, Margaret, Patsy, and me.

Mama, I love you!
May you sense my deep appreciation
through the pages of My Heart's at Home.
After all, you are the one who showed me the true meaning of motherhood.

Contents

Contents

Contents

PREFACE

My Heart's at Home was born years ago when I attended an Arkansas Writers' Conference. When the speaker said that everyone has at least one book in their hearts, I knew that mine would have to address working Christian moms who were committed to their families.

As a wife and mother of two young boys, I was juggling home and work responsibilities, and I needed some help. There were books about a woman's walk with Christ, motherhood, and careers. But I could not find even one aimed specifically at helping the Christian working mom balance her many roles—keeping her relationships with the Lord and her family as priorities.

The journey of *My Heart's at Home* has had many forks in the road. It was only after I completely gave my writing desires to the Lord that he undoubtedly opened his door for this book to become a reality. While I was working one day at FamilyLife (a division of Campus Crusade for Christ), a colleague of mine, John Kriz, mentioned that there really needed to be a book for the working Christian mom. I explained to him that this had been a dream of mine for years and that I had already started a manuscript. He said that he and his wife, Lori, would love to read it. John gave my incomplete manuscript to Mike Petersen, who gave it to Ken Stephens of Broadman & Holman Publishers, who then brought it to the attention of Bucky Rosenbaum and Len Goss.

I believe that "God's people always have God's provision in God's time." Although I felt quite inadequate while writing the final manuscript, my friend Phyllis Baize reminded me of the words of Philippians 1:6, "He who began a good work in you will carry it on to completion until the day of Christ Jesus." Knowing that Christ had truly opened the door for this book, I found great comfort when I recognized that he would guide me.

May God receive the glory!

Acknowledgments

Psalm 100 reminds us to give thanks to the Lord. I realize that God orchestrated the writing of *My Heart's at Home*, for which I am very grateful.

I truly appreciate my editor, Leonard Goss, for his encouragement and help, for believing in me, and for wanting to help working Christian moms.

John and Lori Kriz, and Mike and Joan Petersen—God undoubtedly used all of you in the publication journey of *My Heart's at Home*. Thank you from the depths of my heart.

I'm also very grateful for the ongoing prayers and encouragement of my husband, Jim; sons, Chris and John; Sunday school class (Little Rock's First Baptist Church); and many friends at FamilyLife. Surely your prayers were the fuel for this book!

Many thanks to the Arkansas Pen Women whose mentoring encouraged me to think that even I could attempt writing a book. Phyllis Baize, Michelle Baxter, Kay Bass, Matt and Lori Burns, Gloria Cates, Julie Denker, Betty Dillon, Merle and Lynn Engle, Kathy Harrill, Jo Ann Henle, Sharon Hill, Arlene Kirk, Glenda Malenke, Elaine Parker, Dennis and Barbara Rainey, Fran Taylor—you were there when *My Heart's at Home* was little more than an idea. Thanks for your encouragement, suggestions, and love.

Anje Anstaett, Barbara Craft, Judi Hurt, Margaret Sarkozi—I don't think anyone could have had a better "reading committee" than the four of you. Thank you for giving your time and talents to help make this book biblical and practical. I appreciate you much more than words can express! May God abundantly bless you and your families!

Janet Greenwood, Rita Looney, Laura Martin, Maury Quo—the stories of how you balance work and family are the shoe leather of this book. You taught me a lot, and I know that you will encourage many other women. Thanks for your transparency and for your willingness to share what God has taught you over the years.

INTRODUCTION

A bell is not a bell
Until you ring it.
A song is not a song
until you sing it.
Love wasn't put
In the heart to stay,
For Love isn't love
Until you give it away.

Some very dear friends of mine, Harry and Harriet Powell, gave me a plaque more than twenty years ago with the above inscription. I think its message is especially meaningful to working mothers. I love my husband and children so very much, and yet that love must be shown daily in tangible ways. Silent thoughts won't convey my love. As a working mom, I need all of the help I can get to maximize my time with my family.

My husband, Jim, and I have two wonderful boys, Chris and John. We pray that their lives will exemplify Christ in all they do. We have also parented several foster children and a niece throughout the years. So, as a busy wife and mother, I

1

know how tough it is to juggle responsibilities at home with those of the office.

I've written this book to encourage working moms. We can never be Super Mom—she just does not exist. But we can be committed Christian women whose hearts are at home.

Possibly you have always worked outside the home, or maybe you just became employed after your youngest began school. You might identify with one of my sisters who is struggling as a single mom trying to raise responsible kids. But because you are reading this book, I envision you as a mother who really wants to put God and her family before her career.

Through the printed page we'll visit with married working mothers and with those who juggle home and work responsibilities as single moms. We'll not only learn some things that can help us maximize our time, but will also get to know some very special ladies who will share their lives with us.

This book will not deal with whether it is right or wrong for women to work outside the home. That is for you and your family to consider prayerfully before God. I hope that this book, however, will bring us back to what is really important. It is not a clean house, washed clothes, or time management, but rather our relationship with God and with our loved ones.

I once heard someone say, "Love can't be paid back; it can only be passed on." It is up to you and me, as moms, to pass Christ's love to the next generation. It takes commitment to keep our hearts at home and to focus on what is really important.

Let's spend some time together getting acquainted. Let's see how we can organize the seemingly never-ending tasks at home to maximize the time that we do have with our families. Let's link arms with other working women and see how we can instill values and character in our children. Together we will learn how to write our own creeds as working mothers and together we will look to a sovereign Lord who controls everything.

You are probably reading this book after a long day at the office. So go ahead, get a cup of steaming hot coffee or refreshing tea. Sit down. Relax. Prop up those feet as we journey together to keep our hearts at home.

I pray that God will use this time to encourage you and your family. May you and I be women whose lives radiate the love we have for our homes.

CHAPTER 1

THE GREAT JUGGLING ACT

*A wife of noble character who can find? She is worth far
more than rubies. Her husband has full confidence in her
and lacks nothing of value. She brings him good, not harm,
all the days of her life. She selects wool and flax and works
with eager hands. She is like the merchant ships, bringing
her food from afar. She gets up while it is still darkness; and
she provides food for her family and portions for her servant
girls. She considers a field and buys it; out of her earnings
she plants a vineyard. She sets about her work vigorously;
her arms are strong for her tasks. She sees that her trading is
profitable, and her lamp does not go out at night. . . .*

*Her children arise and call her blessed; her husband also,
and he praises her; "Many women do noble things, but you
surpass them all." Charm is deceptive, and beauty is fleeting;
but a woman who fears the Lord is to be praised. Give her
the reward she has earned, and let her works bring her
praise at the city gate.*

PROVERBS 31:10–18, 28–31

The Proverbs 31 woman inspires awe. How did she do it?
How did she balance her vigorous work schedule with her de-
votion to family?

If she were a working woman of the nineties, we might imagine her totally devoted to her husband and children, having a flexible full-time job that still allowed her the time to sew all of the family's clothes—even to tailor her husband's suits. She would talk on her cellular phone to her PTA committee chairman while working in her massive garden (of course, she would give most of the vegetables to the poor). And no doubt she also would home-school her ten children. No wonder her lamp did not go out!

Is activity the message of Proverbs 31? I think not. This woman was not honored because of her accomplishments; she was valued because of her noble character (v. 10). She brought good all the days of her life. Could her numerous activities have taken place over the years, even decades of her lifetime? As a working wife and mother, I want to know how she juggled so many responsibilities. Since she received blessings from her children and praises from her husband, she must have made a positive impact on her family. What was her secret? She feared the Lord. Her hope was in him!

Scripture tells us that "the fear of the LORD is the beginning of wisdom" (Prov. 9:10). Yes, God is sovereign. He is the same yesterday, today, and tomorrow (Heb. 13:8). No matter what the situation in which we find ourselves, if we put our trust in God first, he will give us needed wisdom for family and work responsibilities.

We both know that it is tough to juggle home and work responsibilities as married Christian mothers. And it is even tougher for those who find themselves raising children alone. Regardless of your marital status, I believe the number one way we can keep our priorities straight is to trust God and heed the leading of his Spirit through his Word.

Sometimes I imagine myself as one of the Israelites whom Pharaoh just freed from Egypt (Exod. 14). Although I know that God is all-powerful and in control, the Egyptians are marching after me. And there is simply nowhere to go—no escape—only the Red Sea.

Let's go to Exodus 14:13–14 where Moses told the Israelites not to be afraid. "Stand firm," he said, "and you will see the deliverance the Lord will bring you today. The Egyptians you see today you will never see again. The Lord will fight for you; you need only to be still."

Moses did not say that the Israelites should run, or jump, or call out to the Lord in loud voices. His words were: "You need only to be still." This advice is as true today as it was centuries ago.

There was no place for the Israelites to go. Only the Red Sea was straight ahead with its treacherous waters. And then God did the impossible. He parted the sea.

As a working mom, I often feel like I am in the middle of an impossible balancing act, and yet the impossible is God's specialty. "Lord," I say, "I'm at my Red Sea. I need to see your hand part some waters." And do you know what? Very often he does just that! It might be in the form of a friend offering to bring the kids home from a practice, or in the guise of a thoughtful husband preparing dinner. But it has usually been in a quiet voice reminding me that his strength is indeed sufficient (2 Cor. 12:9–10).

In Joshua 3:7, the Lord said to Joshua, "I am with you as I was with Moses." As the Lord was with Joshua, so he is with us.

I had planned on being a stay-at-home mom. Our first child, Christopher, was born about the same time my husband became self-employed. When Chris was eight months old, I needed to return to work—for supposedly a year or so. Then came private Christian schooling. What was to be one year turned into two and then into ten and now into twenty.

But with the Lord's grace, even though I've had to work throughout their lives, somehow our boys are doing well. They both love the Lord, excel in athletics, are smart, handsome, and have leadership qualities. (Now, don't I sound like their mom?) Jim and I pray that they will put Christ first for their entire lives.

I recall times when John, even as a little boy, reminded us to stop and pray about something that concerned our family. And I vividly remember Chris writing on the back of a poster why he knew that he was a Christian. Years later, I was proud to call a young man with a shaved head my son. Some college acquaintances had challenged him to either get drunk or have his head shaved. He said with a smile, "Bring out the clippers."

I marvel at how the Lord's hand has been on our sons. Although at times I have wondered what might have been had I been a stay-at-home mom, I know God was not taken by surprise by the forks in the road of my life. There is great comfort to all Christian working moms in Romans 8:28: "And we know that in all things God works for the good of those who love him, who have been called according to his purpose."

The same Lord who parted the Red Sea has guided our family and parted the waters for us time and time again. He has used a mom and dad who have made lots of mistakes to mold two wonderful young men. I believe that the Lord still can, and does, part the water for his children. But we need to be watching and waiting. For the waters quickly part only to unite again, when once more we see the endless sea.

Yes, we must be still and watch the hand of the mighty Lord at work today in our lives and in our families.

Shortly after our older son Chris was born, I wrote: "I hope Christopher will see life and God's glory in the tiniest rose petal and in the smallest of animals. When he is old enough to walk with me in the yard, I will hold his small hands up to the sun, into the soil of the earth, and over the grass. I will show him the miracles of life. But the greatest miracle of life to me will be my son—my son, Christopher!"

Moms, we must spend time in prayer and in God's Word in order to receive needed wisdom to nurture our children. I am reminded of a story our pastor once told about a lumberjack who was hired because he was strong and committed to his task. When this young man was first hired, he cut down more trees than anyone else. When the other lumberjacks took breaks, he didn't. He would skip lunch and work until there was no longer light.

Then the young man's production began to dwindle. Realizing that he was not taking breaks, his boss confronted him about the need to pause from the hectic pace of chopping trees. The young man did not heed his suggestion, claiming that he did not have time for such refreshment.

In time, the boss once again came up to the young man and put his arm around his shoulder. The young man imagined words of commendation about his diligent work. But rather than praise, his boss said that his services were no longer needed.

"You are firing me?" he uttered in disbelief. "Haven't I worked longer and harder than anyone else, and taken virtually no breaks?"

"Yes, this is true," was the response. "But when did you sharpen your ax?"

You see, this foreman knew that a dull ax meant fewer downed trees and a potential deadly accident. Not a good situation to be in.

Mom, do you and I take needed time to sharpen our axes? Do we prayerfully ask God to give us wisdom concerning the hours we work and the ways we nurture our children and love our husbands? If not, we are accidents about to happen—costly accidents that could take the form of shattered relationships where they count the most—at home.

God will be faithful, but we must take time to sharpen our axes with his Word and with prayer. A little card I have says,

"The task before me is never greater than the power within me." These words are both comforting and convicting.

As a working mom, life is an especially challenging juggling act, and yes, I have often dropped some balls. But when I keep my focus on Christ and his purpose for my family, the act becomes far easier to execute. After all, as Paul said in 2 Corinthians 12:10, "That is why, for Christ's sake, I delight in weaknesses. . . . For when I am weak, then I am strong."

SCRIPTURES FOR REFLECTION

Trust in the Lord with all your heart and lean not on your
own understanding; in all your ways acknowledge him,
and he will make your paths straight.

PROVERBS 3:5–7

Read about the godly woman in Proverbs 31.

By wisdom a house is built, and through understanding it is
established; through knowledge its rooms are filled
with rare and beautiful treasures.

PROVERBS 24:3–4

But seek first his kingdom and his righteousness,
and all these things will be given to you as well.

MATTHEW 6:33

QUESTIONS TO PONDER

1. The Proverbs 31 woman was revered because she feared the Lord, not because of her deeds. How do I show that I fear the Lord?

2. How much time do I spend daily with the Lord in his Word and prayer? What changes (if any) do I need to make in my schedule to make this a top priority?

3. How does my life reveal whether my deeds are for God's glory or mine?

4. What are some of the rare and beautiful treasures that I desire for my home and family? How do they compare with God's desire for my home and family? (Some of mine are a solid marriage, children of godly character, a living faith in Christ, and a willingness to admit mistakes and ask forgiveness.)

CHAPTER 2

HOW TO MAKE HOME A PRIORITY

The Christian life is not a playground; it is a battleground.

WARREN WIERSBE

"Mom, it's raining outside."
"Mom, Jimmy won't leave me alone."
"Mom, Debbie won't get out of the shower."
"Mom, what's for dinner?"

If you are working outside of the home and have children, you likely have received calls at work with messages similar to these. What's a mother to do? How can you let your kids know that they are a priority even though you are working?

One day I jotted down a silly poem that captures some of the juggling that we working moms do, while trying to maintain home as a priority:

She awakens at five on the dot,
To the old alarm clock.
Drags out of bed,
With a feeling of dread,
For there are dishes to wash,
And towels to fold,
And coffee to drink,
Before it gets cold.

She cooks eggs for her crew,
Signs papers for school,
Gives hubby a kiss,
And has her day's to-do list.

Then she packs the lunches at exactly 7:05,
And is off in a flash—for the carpool ride.
The kids take a moment for prayer,
Just about the time Timothy pulls Susie's hair,
Arriving at school, not a moment to lose,
She has only five minutes to put on hat number two.

She's at work by eight,
Doesn't want to be late,
And the day's such a blur, she hardly can see,
When it's time for this lady to put on
Hat number three.

As she walks through the door,
The question she dreads,
The one that makes her feel
Heavier than lead,
You know the one—
When you are really beat,
It's when junior asks: "What's there to eat?"

But there is hope! I believe that God can help us redeem the time that we do have with our children. He will show us how we can tangibly express love to our sons and daughters and make time with our children really count.

I realize that you may be a single mom or that your husband may not be a Christian. If so, you probably feel a tremendous responsibility in raising your children. Remember what God said to Joshua in Joshua 1:5: "I will never leave you nor forsake you." In verse 7 he reminded Joshua to "be strong and very courageous." I think God says these words very tenderly to single and struggling moms. The God of the universe, the Lord of lords, King of kings, and weaver of our beings will never, no NEVER, leave us! And it is never too late to turn to him for guidance.

Let me share a few ways I've tried to make home a priority. (Please understand that they are not listed in any particular order.) Hopefully you will glean an idea or two that will help you with your balancing act.

SHOW OUR CHILDREN HOW MUCH WE LOVE THEM

Live a life of love.
EPHESIANS 5:2

My command is this: Love each other as I have loved you.
JOHN 15:12

But God demonstrates his love for us in this:
While we were still sinners, Christ died for us.
ROMANS 5:8

What great memories I have of a little game my sons and I shared when they were small. "How much do I love you?" I would ask. Then I would begin the game of showing how much. With hands close together, I'd ask, "This much?" They'd laugh and I'd open my hands a bit more. The game would continue until my hands were stretched behind my back as far as possible. Then I'd say, "As much, as much, as much." The boys would laugh and I'd hug them.

Also, when our children were little and I was holding one of their hands, I'd often squeeze it three times. This was our "secret code" for "I love you." They'd squeeze back four times for "I love you, too." Even when the boys became teenagers (although they would never have admitted it), they still appreciated this expression of love.

Of course, hugs and kisses are great ways to show affection. A hug or pat on the back can go a long way with both a little child and a tired teenager. We try to always tell our kids how much we love them whenever they are leaving the house, realizing that we do not know what tomorrow will bring.

An easy way to let our children know they are in our thoughts is by leaving notes in their school lunch boxes. Remind them that you are praying for their test, or basketball try-out, or class election. Let them know that although you are not physically with them during the day, you are with them in your thoughts and prayers.

Even more important, we need to remind our children of Jesus' love for them. I recall a friend, Patty Harris, who asked her little girl, "How much does Mommy love you?" Hannah replied, "As much as Jesus." Patti said she was awestruck to think that her daughter equated her motherly love to God's perfect love. And yet, isn't this true? Our children do see God through us as parents. It is so important for us not only to tell them of our love, but to show this love day-by-day. You and I know this is not always easy after a long day at work. But doesn't God know our circumstances? Can't his love flow through us even when we are tired?

And sometimes we can show our love as we are willingly inconvenienced for our kids. If you have flexibility at work, I strongly encourage you to go on class field trips, help serve the pizza at lunch, and attend school assemblies during the day.

Our children notice our involvement. One of our sons is not as verbal in his feelings as the other. But I will always remember one day when I volunteered to help his class serve chili at lunch for their fund-raiser. Much to my surprise this big teenager put his arm around my shoulder (at school, no less) and told me how much he appreciated my being there. I hit payday when he did that!

There is such encouragement for moms in 1 Thessalonians 5:16–18, "Be joyful always; pray continually; give thanks in all circumstances, for this is God's will for you in Christ Jesus."

MAKE FAMILY A PRIORITY

Children, obey your parents in the Lord, for this is right.

EPHESIANS 6:1

The wise woman builds her house,
but with her own hands the foolish one tears hers down.

PROVERBS 14:1

I will walk in my house with blameless heart.

PSALM 101:2B

Whenever possible, let your children know how much you love their father. Jim and I usually spend some time together before supper catching up on the day's events. I believe this gives the kids security. They see their parents as a team whom God has entrusted with their upbringing. (If you are separated from your husband, remember, he is still your children's father. God does not want you to tear him down to your children with your words.)

We generally eat dinner together, although this has been harder as the kids have gotten older. Sometimes we may not eat dinner until 9 or 9:30 p.m. But to our busy family, a little indigestion is a fair tradeoff for fellowship.

We also attend one another's activities as a family. Having boys, I sometimes feel like one sport rolls into another, and I don't even notice that the year is actually divided into four seasons. To our family, the seasons are not marked by changing leaves and falling snow, but instead by football, basketball, baseball, and track.

We plan family outings such as camping trips, attending local festivals, picking apples at orchards, choosing our pumpkin from a local pumpkin patch, cutting our Christmas tree, riding trains, visiting museums—the list is endless. The important thing is to spend time together!

When Chris was preparing to return to college one fall, he and John went camping in a state park not too far from our home. They really couldn't understand why in the world Jim and I drove over an hour just to join them one evening for a cookout. But you see, this mom missed her boys and needed some "family time" whether they did or not.

It had not rained in nearly three weeks, but—you guessed it—that evening the rains came, and came, and came. Nevertheless, we reached the campsite just in time to help put the guys' baseball gloves and guitar in a dry place before the heavens opened up. Although our steaks were a bit soggy (and the potatoes never did cook completely), we had a great evening together and made some good memories. It may take a little effort to carve out family time, but the dividends are immeasurable—whether the kids are young or almost grown.

LOVE UNCONDITIONALLY

Your attitude should be the same as that of Christ Jesus.
PHILIPPIANS 2:5

My command is this: Love each other as I have loved you.
JOHN 15:12

*But I say to you: Love your enemies, and
pray for those who persecute you.*
MATTHEW 5:44 NASB

Be sure that your children know that you love them for who they are, not for what they do. I'll always remember an outbreak of cheating that took place one year when I taught sixth grade. These children needed to heed the words of Proverbs 10:9, "The man of integrity walks securely, but he who takes crooked paths will be found out." So, as a consequence for the kids' actions, I had those who had cheated write letters to their parents. Let me share three of them with you:

Dear Mom and Dad,

During the spelling test I cheated by changing my answer. I feel really bad and am very sorry for what I did. I feel stupid. I've been feeling pressure from home and that's why I did it.

Dear Mom and Dad,

I cheated on a reading quiz about two weeks ago and gave myself a grade I shouldn't have gotten. I guess the reason I did it is I wanted to please both of you. Even if it meant to cheat on a test. I know you would rather me get an "F" than to cheat on a test and get a good grade. I am sorry for what I did.

Dear Mom,

I got caught cheating. More than one-third of the people in my class got caught. I'm sorry that I did what I did. It was wrong. . . . I get to visit the principal. Sometimes I feel pressure from the class and home. . . .

Sometimes our kids are feeling pressure to do, to perform, to achieve. As parents we should encourage them *to be*—to be the special person God designed them to be. Psalm 139:13–14 reminds us of the unique qualities of each child: "For you created my inmost being, you knit me together in my mother's womb, I praise you because I am fearfully and wonderfully made." As parents, we need to love our kids for who they are, not what they do.

Obviously, this has to be balanced. One of our children once announced that he did not do too well on a test. "Exactly how did you do?" Jim asked. The reply was "Well, it was a high F." At least our son was optimistic. And with a reduction in activities, his grades turned out just fine at the end of the year. We didn't love him less because of his grade, but we knew he was capable of much more than "high F's."

Our sons have generally excelled in sports. But one particular summer really stands out. One of the boys sat on the bench most of the baseball season. This was really hard for him and for us, as he was used to playing all of the time. But Jim and I made a commitment to be at his games to support *him,* not his activity. In retrospect, I think our standing by this son in his trying season was probably more important than it had been in his "days of glory." I believe our mere presence at these particular games said loud and clear that we love our sons because of who they are, not because of their achievements.

Finally, I am so glad that God doesn't mark me down a notch when I mess up. I have fallen short many times, such as when I raised my voice instead of listening, wasn't patient, overreacted, didn't wait on God, etc. I really need to show my kids the same grace that the Lord has so freely shown me when I have failed him. For only then can I unconditionally love my children with Christ's perfect love and show them a tangible picture of 1 Corinthians 13:5: "[Love] keeps no record of wrongs."

COMMUNICATE, COMMUNICATE, COMMUNICATE

A word aptly spoken is like apples of gold in settings of silver.
PROVERBS 25:11

These commandments that I give you today are to be upon your hearts. Impress them on your children. Talk about them

*when you sit at home and when you walk along the road,
when you lie down and when you get up.*

DEUTERONOMY 6:6–7

*Teach them to your children, talking about them when you
sit at home and when you walk along the road, when you lie
down and when you get up.*

DEUTERONOMY 11:19

As working moms, it is so important for us to communicate while we are preparing breakfast, packing lunches, or driving to and from the day care or school.

When I would drive the kids to school, we would take turns being prayer warriors. Chris and John would pray for Jim and my day at work and for their day at school. We found this to be a great way not only to start our mornings, but also to know what was on the boys' hearts.

Yet sometimes our family seems to be headed in a million different directions. Sound familiar? I imagine you can identify. That's why we started weekly meetings several years ago, and this has really helped with communication. Each of us has our own calendar. We write in school activities, work responsibilities, church functions, and social plans. This has prevented many misunderstandings.

For a time, one of our sons had a hard time keeping up with school assignments and outside activities. It helped for him to write his day's assignments and activities on a small note card, and he crossed them off when they were finished. Since he was a teenager, we added a little incentive. We gave him $1 for every completed card that he gave Jim or me before he went to bed. One dollar a day seemed a much smaller price than nagging parents and incomplete work.

Communication is especially critical as children get older. We will soon have two sons in college, and I cannot stress enough the importance of communicating genuine expectations. Over the years, Jim and I have found that misunderstandings around activities often occur when we do not clearly review calendars.

I remember once when we declared one Saturday, "Family Work Day." Jim's and my intentions were that the entire family would work that entire Saturday. After all, it was a work *day*. But this was not what one of our teenagers thought. He had planned on working just half of a day, and then going fishing with his buddies. Needless to say, he was not a happy camper and neither were Jim and I. All of this could have been avoided if we had clearly explained that we needed to pull together as a family and do yard work for the entire Saturday.

Jim and I occasionally write our kids notes of encouragement. They will generally receive letters from us on their birthdays, the first day of school, and on special holidays. When they were small, they would often find a note tucked into their school lunches. Even today, it is not unusual for them to discover a note on the kitchen counter reminding them that we will be praying about a big test or thanking them for a chore well done.

We also have had "good news/bad news" at the dinner table for as long as I can remember. Each of us shares the best and the worst things that have happened during our day. Sometimes we are overjoyed with an award one of the kids has won. Other times we ache with their disappointments. I will always remember one evening when one of the boys told us that the school secretary's husband had been murdered and another commented that a young lady whom I once taught was thinking of having an abortion. These were big—no, huge—issues that required loving action.

Ask your kids questions and honor their God-given individuality. When I picked John up from football practices, I wanted to know all about his school days and practice. After many afternoons of one-syllable answers, I asked John if he liked to talk when I picked him up. He said, "No." He then went on to say that he needs to be quiet when he is exhausted from practice, and would really appreciate my not asking him so many questions. This certainly goes against my talkative nature, but I decided that I needed to put his needs above mine. I have found that in the evening, after John has rested and eaten, he is much more willing to talk.

Jim and I will often drop by our sons' rooms at night just to see how their day has been. Sometimes they will really open up and talk, and talk, and talk. As parents, we need to be available even if it means we'll get a little less sleep. And I will be the first to admit that this is not always easy to do after a long day. But who said demonstrating love is easy?

My sister Margaret, who is raising her children as a single mom, told me how especially important it is for single moms to spend one-on-one time with their children. She sets aside special days with each of her two children for just this purpose and tries to join them in activities that they like.

Author Miriam Neff has developed an excellent exercise for parents to do with their teens. I think it could be adapted for elementary children as well, and I would like to share it with you:

"How Well Do You Know Your Teenager?"
by Miriam Neff*

1. Who is your teen's best friend?

2. What color would he/she like for the walls in his/her bedroom?

3. Who is your teen's greatest hero?

---

* Taken from the "FamilyLife Today" resource "How Well Do You Know Your Teenager?" "FamilyLife Today" is the radio program of FamilyLife, a division of Campus Crusade for Christ.

4. What embarrasses your teen most?

5. What is your teen's biggest fear?

6. What is his/her favorite type of music?

7. What person outside the immediate family has most influenced your teen?

8. What is his/her favorite school subject?

9. What is his/her least favorite school subject?

10. What has your teen done that he/she feels most proud of?

11. What is your teen's biggest complaint about the family?

12. What sport does your teen most enjoy?

13. What is his/her favorite TV program?

14. What really makes your teen angry?

15. What would your teen like to be when he/she grows up?

16. What chore does your teen like least?

17. What three foods does your teen like most?

18. What is your teen's most prized possession?

19. What is his/her favorite family occasion?

20. What activity did your teen enjoy most last weekend?

Communication—how important it is! But let's face it, after a hard day at work too often it is easy to respond with a sharp word—one that would not glorify God. I have asked the Lord to help me communicate with his love and grace. When I want to react in the flesh, often I seem to hear a little voice say "testing, testing." Proverbs 15:1 tells us that "A gentle answer turns away wrath." Will I pass the test and give a gentle answer? Will my words be like those described in Proverbs 25:11: "A word aptly spoken is like apples of gold in settings of silver"? The choice is up to me.

EVALUATE ACTIVITIES

Choose for yourselves this day whom you will serve. . . .
But as for me and my household, we will serve the LORD.

JOSHUA 24:15

I, wisdom, dwell together with prudence;
I possess knowledge and discretion.

PROVERBS 8:12

There is a time for everything,
and a season for every activity under heaven.

ECCLESIASTES 3:1

This is a tough one—especially as the kids have gotten older. There are countless activities vying for our family's time. And honestly, sometimes our family overschedules and we have to weed out some of our commitments. After all, if we are trying to create a peaceful, loving home, we have to spend time there—at home.

We should prayerfully ask the Lord to show us our children's bents so we will be able to discern which activities are best for them. When we had five children in our household, the kids were limited in their personal activities. They simply had to take turns doing various things unless they could be involved in the same activity at the same time.

Even though I am a Christian mom who is working outside the home, I really want the best for Jim and my kids and desire to give them the opportunities they truly need. Once, after teaching all year, I was so excited about the approach of summer because I was going to be sure that our sons could excel in their many talents—for their good, of course. We had swimming lessons, baseball practices, art lessons, tennis lessons, and naturally, piano lessons. As a teacher, I was looking forward to "being home" with the kids. I was willing to chauffeur them anywhere for their summer fun. Then one day one of our boys said that he just wanted to stay home. He wanted to play baseball and enjoy summer at our house. He didn't want to go to activity after activity.

Do you know what we did? We listened to him. We pulled the plug on activities and let him be a little boy who built forts in the backyard and climbed trees—a little boy who got to know the other children in the neighborhood and enjoyed walking his dog. My mother used to tell me to enjoy being a kid. "You'll only be a child once," she would say. Even today her advice is good—very good!

That summer I learned that we cannot do it all—and that includes our kids. Ecclesiastes 3 reminds us that there is a time for everything. *We are still learning this.* Helping your kids prioritize activities is not easy! Especially if you have many children who want to be involved in many activities.

My prayer is that you and I will be especially sensitive to God's priorities for our families in his perfect timing. We have all made mistakes and there is no perfect mother. But what does it profit a mom if her son is the president of the United States or an NFL football player, but loses his soul. Godly character is far more valuable than activities and honors.

PRAY, PRAY, PRAY

We do not know what we ought to pray for,
but the Spirit himself intercedes for us with groans
that words cannot express.
ROMANS 8:26B

Pray that you will not fall into temptation.
LUKE 22:40B

*What other nation is so great as to have their gods
near them the way the LORD our God is near us
whenever we pray to him?*

DEUTERONOMY 4:7

When the children were little, Jim and I would take one-on-one time to read them stories and say bedtime prayers. But as they grew older, the one-on-one prayer time changed into a family prayer time. As a family, we still kneel at one of our sons' beds and pray together. It means a lot to me when our teenaged son willingly gets off the phone after he has told one of his friends that it is time for him to pray with his family.

We pray before meals, joining hands and thanking God for the food with which he has blessed us. And Jim and I also pray together before we go to bed. We ask God to put a hedge of protection around our sons, that they will have Christian friends, that their future spouses will love the Lord, and that they will be lights in this dark world.

We do try to make prayer a natural part of our day. If Jim and I have special challenges at work, or the boys have a problem, we try to stop in the midst of our turmoil and seek God's direction. Yes, sometimes I forget to do this and I am so humbled when one of the boys asks, "Have you prayed?"

Recently I was privileged to go on a missions trip to Mexico with our son John. He and a group of kids had gotten off a bus in an unfamiliar Mexican neighborhood—one they knew they should not be in alone. What were they to do? They could not speak Spanish!

The group became divided. Some of the kids thought they knew the way back to the institute where we were staying and started walking. But the other group stopped and huddled together in a circle, and our John led them in prayer. No sooner had they finished praying than a Spanish woman pulled up to them who "happened" to speak English. She asked if the kids were lost and they said they sure were. When they told her where they were staying, she replied that the woman who lived there was one of her closest friends, and she drove the kids back to where they belonged.

I hate to tell you this, but too often I identify with the kids who chose to walk back in a foreign land. But to the group seeking God's direction, he provided what I believe was divine guidance. He had already prepared a good work for the English-speaking woman. Through prayer and her obedience, the Lord was glorified, and I was once again reminded of the power of prayer and the importance of trusting God.

I also pray that even though God has given me a wonderful job, he'll keep my heart at home. I want my home to remain my priority. Dale Hanson Bourke captured this spirit in "What Motherhood Really Means" (*Reader's Digest,* February 1991, p. 193–94):

> . . . I look at her manicured nails and stylish suit and think that no matter how sophisticated she is, becoming a mother will reduce her to the primitive level of a bear protecting her cub. That an urgent call of "Mom!" will cause her to drop her best crystal without a moment's hesitation.
>
> I feel I should warn her that no matter how many years she has invested in her career, she will be professionally derailed by motherhood. She might arrange for child care, but one day she will be going into an important business meeting, and she will think about her baby's sweet smell. She will have to use every ounce of discipline to keep from running home, just to make sure her child is all right. . . .
>
> Looking at my attractive friend, I want to assure her that eventually she will shed the pounds of pregnancy, but she will never feel the same about herself. That her life, now so important, will be of less value to her once

she has a child. That she would give it up in a moment to save her offspring, but she will also begin to hope for more years—not to accomplish her own dreams, but to watch her child accomplish his.

* * *

Let's turn once again to Proverbs 31:

> *A wife of noble character who can find?*
> *She is worth far more than rubies.*
> *Her husband has full confidence in her*
> *and lacks nothing of value.*
> *She brings him good, not harm,*
> *all the days of her life. . . .*
> *Her children arise and call her blessed;*
> *her husband also, and he praises her:*
> *"Many women do noble things,*
> *but you surpass them all."*
> *Charm is deceptive, and beauty is fleeting;*
> *but a woman who fears the LORD is to be praised.*
> *Give her the reward she has earned,*
> *and let her works bring her praise at the city gate.*

PROVERBS 31:10–12, 28–31

May you and I apply the scriptural principles that speak of godly love, the family, communication, time management, and prayer. How reassuring it is to know that God will continuously sharpen us through his Word and equip us with his wisdom.

May our children one day arise and call us blessed. If we are married, may our husbands praise us. May we fear the Lord and praise him through the lives he has entrusted to us. There could be no greater legacy than this.

SCRIPTURE FOR REFLECTION

> *There is a time for everything,*
> *and a season for every activity under heaven:*

a time to be born and a time to die,
a time to plant and a time to uproot,
a time to kill and a time to heal,
a time to tear down and a time to build,
a time to weep and a time to laugh,
a time to mourn and a time to dance,
a time to scatter stones and a time to gather them,
a time to embrace and a time to refrain,
a time to search and a time to give up,
a time to keep and a time to throw away,
a time to tear and a time to mend,
a time to be silent and a time to speak,
a time to love and a time to hate,
a time for war and a time for peace.

ECCLESIASTES 3:1–8

QUESTIONS TO PONDER

1. What are my priorities for today? How do they match God's priorities for me?

For this month?

For this year?

For life?

2. How does my schedule reflect these priorities?

3. What one thing can I do today that will help me focus
   on meeting God's priorities for my life?

CHAPTER 3

TAKE TIME TO MAKE MEMORIES

We have this moment to hold in our hand,
And to touch as it slips through our fingers like sand.
Yesterday's gone and tomorrow may never come,
But we have this moment today!

GLORIA GAITHER AND SHIRLEY DOBSON,

LET'S MAKE A MEMORY

The Lord was so good when he gave Jim and me our boys. I had difficulty delivering both of them, so we recognized from the beginning that their lives were truly God's gifts to us. (As Psalm 127:3 says, "Sons are a heritage from the Lord, children a reward from him.") We have enjoyed watching them mature and have cherished countless memories over the years.

As a new mom, I vividly recall older mothers telling me how quickly the boys would grow up. I knew that they were right, but somehow in the midst of changing diapers and rocking babies, that "someday" seemed far, far away. Now I am that older mother looking back in awe, wondering where the time went. Friends of mine, Mike and Kaye Rutter, expressed this so well when Mike said that "The years do fly by so quickly, it's just those days that seem to never end when you have little children."

As I share a few tangible ways that we have made lasting family memories, remember that I am a mom with clay feet who has not done it all. There are stacks and stacks of pictures that still need to be placed neatly in scrapbooks. And if something needed to be sewn, the kids usually outgrew whatever needed mending by the time I got to it. And believe me, I will never be given the House Beautiful Award as long as there are children living in our home.

Ecclesiastes 3:1 tells us, "There is a time for everything, and a season for every activity under heaven." As a working mom, I know that your plate is certainly full. But let me challenge you to take the time to make family memories. Dust can wait, but our sons' and daughters' childhoods cannot be recaptured.

WE HAVE TO MAKE THE EFFORT

We have done many things as a family: taken train rides, gone on fishing trips, climbed mountains, taken ferries instead of freeways, dug for diamonds, gone to air shows, explored caves, watched the launching of hot air balloons, held newborn puppies, and marveled at God's sunsets. We've picked pumpkins, peaches, apples, made insect collections and model cars. Once we even saw an exhibition by parachutists and witnessed a Dalmatian jumping from a plane with his master. I would not have believed it had I not been there.

Most of such family outings had a price tag of time instead of money. If you watch the newspapers and network with friends, you can keep abreast of the family activities in your town or city. And don't overlook the art galleries, museums, libraries, and lakes that may be at your own backdoor.

Once I volunteered for a local museum and brought various animals to our children's school. I will never forget the baby alligator that called our bathtub home for the night. And of course, there was also the ferret, mama mouse, owl, and snake. What fun we had as a family when I would bring these unusual house guests home before their trips to school.

Birthdays are great memory-makers. My all-time favorite birthday celebration was when Jim turned thirty-four. The kids had a surprise carnival for him (which was totally their idea). They led him blindfolded to a game room that housed their various booths. They capped the evening off with Jim hitting a piñata filled to the brim with candy. Afterwards we all went out to eat Mexican food. I really do not remember what presents, if any, Jim received that year. But I do recall that the kids had given themselves creatively to show their dad that they loved him.

We've celebrated birthdays with skating, bowling, pizza, and slumber parties. One of my favorite birthday parties was when Chris was only one year old. He was born two months prematurely—actually, he was not expected to live at that time. We invited families who had truly held us up during this ordeal to celebrate his first birthday with us. It was such an encouragement to gather with them! A favorite picture shows Chris being held in the long arm of one of our friends (who looked as though he must have played football in his younger days). As a one-year-old, Chris was totally cradled in this man's long arm. We had taken a picture of Chris being held by this same man when Chris was about five weeks old—he barely filled the man's large hands. Comparing the two pictures still makes us marvel at the wonderful work of the Lord.

Our favorite parties included a cowboy party in our backyard. The little boys came dressed as cowboys, of course. And our big dogs were perfect horses. When John turned twelve he wanted a football party at a local park. After several games of football, we roasted hot dogs and marshmallows and had a wonderful evening. Again, this did not cost a lot of money. It did take a little planning and some time, but the memories were well worth the effort.

Also, have your kids write down their impressions of events. President Reagan visited Little Rock when our boys were quite small—October 27, 1988, to be exact. John, barely eight at the time, wrote his impression of that big day. In the unmistakable penmanship of a child, he said: "Well, this morning I went to see President Reagan. It was very boring. We had to stand for four hours strait. Even thou I got to see him, it was still a little boring. But theres one part when I got to pet the hores. His name was Bow, I think. It was a police hores. It was a new one. So I guess it wasn't so bad."

PICTURES ARE TRULY WORTH A THOUSAND WORDS!

I wish I had a dollar for every picture that we have. We'd be billionaires for sure! But in our hearts we are billionaires with memories. Even the commonplace can be transformed into memory-makers. I recall how a foster child once asked for a horse for Christmas. Although she did not get the horse, she did get a private riding lesson complete with pictures.

The scrapbooks are full of pictures chronicling special occasions—birthdays, holidays, visits from relatives. But we have also taken pictures of everyday life, and I think these might be the most special pictures of all. Building forts, stacking blocks, eating ice cream, hitting a baseball, riding on dad's back, being carried by dad as a "sack of potatoes"—when I see these pictures I recall the love that cements a family together. We always try to keep a camera loaded to capture that unexpected snowstorm (yes, it has happened a time or two in Little Rock) or even a refreshing dance in the warm rain.

We have discovered that it's fun to take both color and black and white pictures. We get triplicates when we have film developed—grandparents and loved ones really enjoy receiving pictures. And we have taken pictures to mark the passing of time: the annual pictures of each child and his teacher, family pictures at Christmas, and the milestone pictures of that first day behind the wheel, and the releasing of a child to college.

We've had a lot of fun going through family albums and have created a "wall of fame" by our staircase. There we see pictures of several generations. When we told the boys that their actions reflected God and the Larmoyeux family, they knew well the faces of those grandparents and great-grandparents who paved their legacy. Of course, at this point, how Chris and John live their lives is up to them. Our prayer is that they will glorify God in all they do!

But I have not been as organized as I would have liked when it comes to pictures. Our scrapbooks are littered with the telltale signs of "sticky notes" where I have taken out pictures over the years for special bulletin boards at school, yearbooks, senior highlights. I wish I had realized that I would rob the kids' scrapbooks in this way. How much better it would have been to have kept an envelope with extra pictures of those "special memories." If they were not returned, it would not have mattered. I also wish I had always written descriptions on the back of pictures. Even today I am not sure of the identities of everyone in various photographs.

We have recorded lots of videotapes of our kids and their grandparents. We rented or borrowed a video camera until we finally bought one for ourselves. At different times, the boys have been given assignments to uncover our family's history. How we cherish the videotapes that we recorded of Jim and my parents where they told of their childhoods and memories.

LETTERS AND AWARDS CHRONICLE LIFE

OK, I confess, I am the all-time pack rat. I have even saved lots of the letters that grandparents and Jim and I have written to the boys for various reasons. They are either neatly mounted in scrapbooks or are in boxes that I will be going through all too soon when our home no longer echoes with the sounds of children.

A few favorite letters that I have saved include:

Dear John,

I'm so proud of you for getting two second place ribbons. When you do your best, it doesn't matter that you didn't come in first. Your efforts make me proud of you like God is proud of you.

> *Dad*

Dear John,

Thank you for the pretty hot pan holder. I use it all the time. In fact, it is my favorite. I have all of your papers. You are a smart little boy, and I am so proud of you. You really make good grades. I liked your mystery story about the dog very much. I also read your papers about God and wisdom. . . .

> *I love you,*
> *Mamoo*

Dear Daddy,

Daddy, you now how you love me? because I love you so much I wanted to give you a present. because I love you so much

> *From John*
> *to Daddy!*

Dear Mom and Dad,

We cannot think of something to sell. Can you help? If you can, write down some idias. Leave them under a rock by your door.

Anonymuos

Dear journal,

I am thankful far my brothers. They are fun to have around and fun to play with. They share their toys with other peiple and like to tickle peiple uner the arm. I love them!

Chris

* * *

And like most households, ours has a varied assortment of awards and trophies that the kids have received—Jim and I have even given the boys a few. When Chris and John were batboys for a baseball team, we got medallions for them. And once, when Chris complained that he had never gotten a trophy for all of his years of basketball, we made a visit to the local trophy store and got him one. His younger brother picked it out and was proud, indeed, to present it to Chris.

But most awards have either found their homes in scrapbooks or are memorialized there through pictures. This has proven handy when trying to remember honors and activities for various applications and forms. I suggest that a mom start a centralized list of awards/honors when her children enter junior high. Had I done this, it would have saved me some valuable time.

RECORD THE MILESTONES

Mom, let's face it, you and I just will not remember the exact dates when our kids first crawled, walked, spoke, became

Christians, were baptized, got their driver's license—the list could go on and on! That's why I have tried to write these things down. I would not have believed that I would forget the dates of such important things—but it happens. So I strongly encourage you to record when baby first walks and talks. You will be glad that you did! I've also tried to record illnesses and injuries in our sons' baby books so I will have one centralized place to go to when I need this information.

As I mentioned earlier, capture milestones in pictures. Magnify the crossroads of your child's life. For example, when our boys were given the keys to the car, it was truly a helpless feeling. I remember hoping that we had trained them right—that they would not only be excellent drivers, but that they would also make the right choices in their cars. Yes, we took pictures on those days, but we also prayed together as a family around their cars—launching the boys into new eras of responsibility.

In addition to putting such pictures in your children's scrapbooks, you may want to consider including your thoughts, prayers, and feelings.

I wish I had begun family Bibles when our sons were infants—ones in which I would have recorded family births, baptisms, and deaths. How wonderful it would be to present such a Bible to each son upon his marriage. It would be a history of God's ongoing work in our family. As the saying goes, it is better late than never, so I may still try to recall the crossroads in our family's life and God's hand of direction through such family Bibles.

When the boys turned thirteen, we asked some of our friends to write them notes of advice concerning their teenage years. Let me share some excerpts:

> Happy 13th! I know this is a special birthday and I think you're ready to become a teenager. . . . I know you have thought through your Christianity and where

you stand with God. God is building strong foundations in your life and I know that He has great plans for you. He wants to use you as a servant/leader in the church and He wants to use you to win others to Him. . . .

Enjoy life because God wants you within the parameters He's given. Thank Him for those boundaries. They are your protection. . . .

• • •

So you have turned thirteen! What a great milestone in your life. You are embarking upon the fabulous experience of manhood. There will be hazards along the way, so keep looking to the Savior and stay in His Word for a successful journey. . . .

• • •

. . . Being 13 is a milestone. I learned something a bit late in life, though I had heard it often. Each day God gives us, including each birthday, well lived, is more important than age, or looks, or size. . . .

• • •

I think of 1 Timothy 4:12 as I consider the years God has ahead for you, "Let no one look down on your youthfulness, but rather in speech, conduct, love, faith, and purity, show yourself an example of those who believe" [NASB].

There will be times when you think too little is expected of you and you will want more, and times when you feel too much is required of you and you will desire less. Yet the goal is to be found obedient and faithful to our God, no matter what He requires of you in whatever particular situation He places before you. I pray that your speech, conduct, love, faith, and purity will deepen in the Lord Jesus so that all through your teen years you will be found to be an example of those who believe. May the Lord continue His work in your heart and may the years ahead be fruitful in His service.

. . .

You are truly one of those special students who I will never forget. I really believe that God has His hand on you and that He has something very special for your life.

. . . As you enter this next stage of your life, my prayer for you is that you will continue to increase "in wisdom and stature, and in favor with God and men" [NASB]—just as Luke 2:52 says that Jesus did as He entered this stage of His life.

* * *

Later, when Chris and John graduated from high school, I surprised them each with a diary that I had kept of their senior year. My father died during Chris's senior year, and I wonder if my thoughts while Dad was so ill might comfort Chris someday when Jim and I are called to our eternal home. And if Chris or John ever question how much their parents love them, all they have to do is pick up their senior diaries.

Upon leaving home for college, Jim and I asked friends to write the boys notes of advice concerning their launch into the world of college. Let me share a few of these letters with you:

. . . God has great plans for you.
1. Stay in the Word of God (Col. 3:16)
2. Obey the Word (James 1:22–25)
3. Honor the Lord (Prov. 3:5–6) . . .

. . .

As you are about to begin this new part of your life remember who you are and live each day as if Christ were standing beside you.

. . .

. . . Maybe the best thing to come out of your senior football season is the realization as to just how important the game is. It is certainly to be played and enjoyed by all those who desire to do so. But it is just a game. However, hopefully, it will teach the participants some extremely valuable things about life. Things like spirit, dedication, commitment, togetherness, adjustment to disappointments, joy as a result of hard work resulting in victory. And hopefully the acceptance of the fact that life goes on regardless as to the outcome of any athletic contest.

• • •

Please always keep God number one in your life. That is all that really matters. The Bible is a treasure. Regard it as such. Learn it, live by it, protect it, and strive to influence others to accept it. They may or may not, but never let that affect the way that Christ, through this inspired Word, affects you, a friend forever. . . .

• • •

As you leave home for college, you will be faced with many new temptations and situations that will challenge your faith. I know that you will remain true to your faith because you have your trust in the Lord. Remember Isaiah 40:28–31. . . .

• • •

Graduation is a beginning of your growth toward adulthood. Continue to keep God and prayer in your life. It works. Your prayers will be answered. . . .

• • •

. . . I challenge you to memorize and live out Proverbs 4:13, "Hold on to instruction, do not let it go; guard it well, for it is your life."

• • •

A whole new chapter of life begins for you soon! My advice for the next few years is to *stay in the Word!* I suggest that each semester, when you register for classes, that you also "register" for a class with the Lord. Select a book of the Scripture or a tape that you will saturate your soul in during that semester. . . .

. . .

. . . Although it will be difficult to bid farewell to this part of your life, go you must into a world in desperate need of a person of faith and strength like you. God be with you! . . . Recognize that the way you live the next fifty years of your life depends on how you want to finish your life. Make your decisions for the present in light of the end goal of righteousness. We desire that you might join Paul in 2 Timothy 4:7–8, "I have fought the good fight, I have finished the race, I have kept the faith." Go forward in Him.

. . .

You are about to embark on one of the most exciting and challenging times in your life. You are about to come to a fork in the road where you must decide something that could mark you for the rest of your life: Are you going to become a mission field? Or a missionary? May God enable you to choose what's right.

* * *

Jim and I hoped that somehow such letters would permeate the hearts and souls of Chris and John with the wisdom of others. I know I have been encouraged today as I pondered the godly advice given to our sons as they entered college. Yes, with Christ, all things are possible.

TO JOURNAL OR NOT TO JOURNAL, THAT IS THE QUESTION

What is journaling? It's simply writing your thoughts down on a regular basis. I have used spiral notebooks and bound journals to record my thoughts. What's important is that you capture what God is teaching you. It will take a little discipline to get into the habit of journaling, but it is worth every bit of the effort.

One of my English teachers challenged our class to journal when I was in the sixth grade. I did so faithfully until I married, and then I just stopped. I began to journal again about six years ago, and it is such fun to recall things that the kids said and did, lessons that the Lord taught me.

The following journal entries are just a few of the precious and meaningful moments that might have been forgotten had I not taken the time to write them down:

4/26: John almost missed a blessing recently. John got in trouble for talking at school and I initially had wanted to side with John rather than his teacher. Jim and I decided that we needed to respect authority and to teach this to John. We had John write his teacher an apology letter (backed by a Bible verse). Mrs. Jackson responded with a wonderful letter to John affirming his Christian leadership.

• • •

10/20: I want to remember John last night. He placed his math book under his pillow in hopes that this somehow would help him in math.

• • •

7/16: Well, he left. Chris really loaded the van and left for the missions trip to inner-city Baltimore. He is out of Jim's and my control. But he's never left God's control.

• • •

7/31: John was so funny the other day. Sunny (his dog) wouldn't get into the backyard. I asked John if he needed a choke chain. He said he just needed a dog that would obey. John said, "I'm the master, he's the dog."

• • •

11/23: Lord, yesterday Chris suffered a mild concussion during football practice. Thank you that he's OK. In a second all of life can change! Help me to honor life constantly and not take it for granted; I praise you for allowing Chris to be OK.

• • •

3/30: I want to remember me telling Carrie that I am going to pray that she's caught when she disobeys and Carrie saying she's going to pray God does not answer my prayers.

• • •

5/8: When a master violinist was playing "Jesus Loves Me" before the church service began, hardly anyone heard it because of talking. I was reminded of how God speaks to us in a still quiet voice. We often don't hear because of our activity.

• • •

6/9: When Jim was fixing the riding mower, his shirt got caught and ripped. It was chewed up by the mower. It could have been his arm. God is good!

• • •

8/1: Lord, it is so good to have both Chris and John back home. It was good to see clutter on John's floor instead of a neat, "kid-free" room. Thank you for the boys. Jim and I pray that they will be men of God.

• • •

8/16: I want to remember getting the plastic worm out of the dryer and John juggling my apples.

· · ·

2/5: Yesterday I poured much love and time into making a cake from scratch. Boy was it delicious! Jim remarked how good it was and asked what mix I used. When I told him it was homemade, he thought he was giving me a compliment when he said, "Well it was good enough to be a mix." (Next time, I'll make a mix.)

· · ·

6/6: Tonight we read Proverbs 31 and when it talked about this woman being worth far more than rubies, John thought it said "RBI's." (For those of you who are not baseball fans, that is "runs batted in.")

* * *

Of course, I could write on and on. How I wish I had written down those funny sayings during the earlier years. So, Mom, is it worth the time to journal? You bet it is!

TRADITIONS ARE IMPORTANT

There is something about traditions that bind a family together. I was taught this clearly when I decided one Thanksgiving that we would have roast beef instead of turkey. Well, our boys were not pleased, to say the least. "It just isn't Thanksgiving," they said. Never again will I make such a mistake.

I am sure that you have some special family traditions of your own. A few of ours include being with relatives during special holidays. We actually cut down a Christmas tree and have the traditional turkey dinner feast for both Thanksgiving and Christmas. And even though the kids have never liked it, we have the tradition of writing thank-you notes for gifts.

Traditions do not need to be limited to holidays. We eat dinner as a family (despite the crazy time) and pray together as a family. These are special traditions. We also took pictures of our children on the first day of every school year. And it just would not be summer without baseball, baseball, and more baseball. Worship has always been important to our family. And while eating Sunday lunch, it has been our tradition to discuss how God used the Sunday sermon in our lives. Every Sunday afternoon, we make our weekly calls to the grandparents. The dictionary defines traditions as habits. What better habit than to make God and family a priority in our everyday lives?

UNEARTHING ROOTS YIELDS RICHES

Ecclesiastes 3:2 tells us that there is "a time to be born and a time to die." No one lives forever, and it is important for our kids to connect with their heritage. What better way than to interview grandmothers and grandfathers. How did they meet? What advice would they like to give their grandkids on dating, marriage, living for the Lord?

Several years ago Jim and I asked our parents to write down their advice to our boys concerning marriage. In their own handwriting they wrote:

> Trust each other. Have a sense of humor. Listen carefully to her side of an argument. Remember the marriage vow, until death do us part. Always be polite, patient, kind, and tolerant. Never go to bed angry. Settle any difference before bedtime. Never carry a resentment.
>
> • • •
>
> Keep your faith in God and be faithful to your marriage vows.
>
> • • •

Papaw and I have always been loyal to each other since we married fifty years ago. All successful marriages need trust. Papaw and I have always trusted each other.

· · ·

A marriage will last and be a joy if you are considerate of each other.

* * *

My dad died several years ago after he and Mom had been married for more than fifty-one years. Jim's parents have been married for more than fifty-four years. We want their advice to be passed on from generation to generation. I am so glad that we asked them to share their thoughts with us while they could.

And thanks to a couple of the boys' history teachers, Chris and John have interviewed their grandparents about serving in the military and about their memories growing up. My mom told them that when she was a little girl Bonnie and Clyde actually stole her parents' car—I had not heard that before. Scrapbooks were opened up, a great-grandfather's book was shared. Memories were passed down that could have been lost forever. And I was amazed when Mom shared her own mother's wedding book that nestled not only her mother's wedding invitation, but also my great-grandmother's wedding invitation from the 1800s.

In this age of photographs, tape-recordings, video cameras, and computers, it is truly easy to capture memories and family histories. These tools can be invaluable in unearthing the roots of those we love.

MAKE SPECIAL MEMORIES TODAY

Our boys always loved to make forts. Some were made by draping a sheet or blanket over chairs. Others were formed with boards and tree limbs. Forts were built in trees, under the house, and in the backyard.

We also kept an "invention" box. Cast-off wheels from cars, small motors, pieces of wood, all would go into the treasured box to be used for some special invention. We tried to help the boys develop creativity by seeing what things could become. Paper towel tubes could be columns for houses, kaleidoscopes, car wheels, etc. Paper plates could become airplanes, and sand and dirt could become "pieces of art."

The kids and I have made many things in the kitchen besides cookies and cakes. A favorite recipe was one for something similar to play dough:

1 cup flour
1/2 cup salt
1 cup water
1 Tablespoon cooking oil
2 teaspoons cream of tartar
Food coloring

Mix all dry ingredients. Add oil, water, and food coloring. Cook over low heat, stirring constantly. Cook until dough becomes one large ball. Empty onto waxed paper. Knead until smooth and cool. Store in an airtight container immediately.

• • •

We'd also bake the following concoction for various ornaments:

1 cup all-purpose flour
1/2 cup salt
Water to mix

Mix and shape into ornaments with a cookie cutter. Bake at 350 degrees until done.

• • •

And the kids always liked rainbow toast:

Put a teaspoon of milk into three cups.
Add a drop of food color in each.
Dip a small brush into each of the milk colors.
Paint a rainbow on a piece of white bread.
Toast the bread, then butter—you have rainbow toast!

* * *

I have found that it is wonderful to have a children's-sized table in the kitchen. Kids can play with puzzles, play dough, etc., while Mom works in the kitchen.

When I was a child, my grandmother would give me sheets of white shelf paper, some glue, and a catalog, and I would cut out my ideal house. This is another fun activity for children to do while you are working around the house.

And take time to record your child's growth on a choice door, wall, or growth chart. I wish that we had begun lining the kids up and marking off their heights at earlier ages. And if I could do it over again, I would also record milestones on the growth chart (first day of kindergarten, high school, when they became Christians, were baptized, etc.).

KEEP YESTERDAY'S MEMORIES

Yes, I am a pack rat extraordinare. But it is worth it when I brush back the pages of time and catch a glimpse of two little boys who have grown up before my eyes.

I have saved many of the boys' school papers over the years.

Once John wrote this list of what he loved:
1. I love Miss Harris!
2. I love animals!
3. I love W.V.C.A.! (his school)

4. I love pizza!!!
5. I love Jesus!!!!!!!
6. I love to play the piano!
7. I love to read.
8. I love Christian music.
9. I love to play in the mud!
10. I love to swim.
11. I love bright colors.
12. I love to sing.
13. I love frogs.

Jim's and my job, as parents, is to help the boys see that in life Jesus is not number five or six, but rather number one. I am still learning this myself!

Yes, yesterday is gone forever. And God does not guarantee us tomorrow. But we do have today. May we invest in our children's lives today and create sweet memories.

Let's review some possible memory makers:

- Watch the local papers to keep abreast of family activities in your area. Remember to visit the art galleries, museums, libraries, and lakes that may be at your own backdoor.
- Creatively celebrate birthdays as a family. Have parties at home with a fun theme (cowboys, carnival night, clowns, sports, tea party).
- Ask the kids to write their impressions of special events. Keep these in a special notebook.
- Keep your camera loaded with film and take pictures of everyday life—building forts, stacking blocks, eating ice cream, hitting a baseball, riding on dad's back, being carried by dad as a sack of potatoes.

- Create a "wall of fame" in your home with pictures of grandparents and great grandparents.
- Keep a special envelope with extra pictures of special memories. You'll need them over the years for bulletin boards, programs, and yearbooks.
- Build an ongoing list of your children's awards and honors. (This will come in handy when completing applications for colleges and scholarships.)
- Record the crossroads in your family's life in a family Bible. Include how God met your needs.
- Keep a diary of your child's senior year and surprise your child with it at graduation.
- Ask special friends and loved ones to write notes of advice to your child concerning their launch into either college or the workplace.
- Write down the funny things that your children say and do while growing up.
- Develop special family traditions.
- Ask the grandparents to write notes of advice about marriage to your children.
- Keep an "invention box." Fill it with things like cast-off wheels from cars, small motors, and pieces of wood.
- Record your child's growth on a wall or wall chart on special days such as birthdays, the first day of school, the day the child becomes a Christian, and the day the child is baptized.

SCRIPTURES FOR REFLECTION

Remember the wonders he has done, his miracles,
and the judgments he pronounced.

1 CHRONICLES 16:12

Remember your Creator in the days of your youth,
before the days of trouble come and the years approach
when you will say, "I find no pleasure in them."

ECCLESIASTES 12:1

I thank my God every time I remember you.

PHILIPPIANS 1:3

QUESTIONS TO PONDER

1. How am I (or my husband and I) consciously making memories for our children?

2. What are our family's traditions?

3. What will my children remember about our home in the mornings, in the evenings, and on Sundays?

4. What can I do to find the time to make memories for my children? (possibly less television, utilizing time spent in the car, better planning, getting help with household chores, etc.)

CHAPTER 4

GOD ONLY GIVES US TWENTY-FOUR HOURS IN A DAY

There is a time for everything,
and a season for every activity under heaven.

ECCLESIASTES 3:1

Come to me, all you who are weary and burdened, and I
will give you rest.

MATTHEW 11:28

Mom, let's face it. As working mothers, a perfectly organized home seems to fit in the same category as fairy tales. There are just not enough hours in the day to do what we often think "must be done." Yet when we look to our Creator, I think we discover that he is the God of organization. As we read in Genesis 1, he created the world in an orderly fashion in six days. After preparing a wonderful universe, God created man on the sixth day and rested on the seventh.

What can you and I learn from this? I believe two things: the importance not only of organization but also of rest. God had a plan—a perfect design for his universe. And after he followed through with his plan, he rested.

Since you are working during much of the day, it is imperative to prioritize those things that, to you, "must" be done. (This list will change according to the age of your children.) With an active family, my top organizational goal is to eat dinner together. This is very important to me because it's at dinner that we connect soul-to-soul with one another. Our mealtime varies depending on our sons' sports schedules and Jim's business appointments. Some nights we may eat at 6 P.M. and others not until 8 P.M. However, with a little advance planning I can organize our household to make family dinners a reality.

You may have a different top priority for your family. Perhaps you have small children and have designated a specific family hour for reading books and playing games. Or maybe your schedule must allow for set activities such as Awana (Approved Workmen Are Not Ashamed) or Scouting.

If you are married, you and your husband should sit down together and decide where you must win, where you can lift one another up, and where you can lose. I cannot begin to tell you how much Jim and I work as a team. Remember, there are only twenty-four hours in a day, and God entrusts our children to us for an unbelievably short time. Our years with our children must be invested in their character—not just spent on mundane chores.

If you are a single Christian mom, remember the words of James 1:5: "If any of you lacks wisdom, he should ask God, who gives generously to all without finding fault, and it will be given to him." God will give you the wisdom you need for each day, if you will seek his will.

Have I done everything perfectly? Absolutely not. I confess that when we were first married, I would often clean the house on Sundays. But Jim convinced me that Sunday is the Lord's day and that I should rest on this one day. After doing so for over two decades, I have found that with rest, God rejuvenates my energy and helps me focus on his desires for our family.

I also remember one Christmas when the mail began to stack up so much that I finally just tossed it into a large laundry basket. It was almost an overwhelming task to finally sort through everything.

And honestly, pictures and scrapbooks have gotten out of control at our house. We literally have boxes of pictures and mementos begging to be placed in scrapbooks. I have had to let them go and realize that all too soon there will be abundant time to organize these precious memories. Although I love to go to seminars on organization and try to glean at least one thing that will help our family, I know I will never reach the mark if it's based on a spotless house and perfectly organized cabinets.

I recall with a smile a story that one of my friends told me. Although she is a working single mom, she pours her life into her children. One night, when she went to give her young son a kiss and say prayers, she actually could not see him because of the toys littering his room.

"Timothy? Timothy? Are you in there?" she asked.

At that point she could have gotten frustrated with the clutter and gone on a mad cleaning spree at the end of a long day. But that night she chose to just stand in the doorway of her son's bedroom and say nighttime prayers. She made the right choice—the lasting choice—the one that emphasized spiritual values rather than an annoyed mom.

I have found that thinking ahead, and organizing what I can, really does help me as a working mom. My prayer is that you will find one or two ideas in this chapter that will enable your home to run more smoothly—not with the hope that you will be an organizational genius, but rather with the desire that you can maximize the time that you do have with your loved ones.

TIME MANAGEMENT

*Be very careful, then, how you live—not as unwise but as
wise, making the most of every opportunity.*

EPHESIANS 5:15

Have weekly meetings where everyone sits down and compares schedules and the upcoming week's activities. Be sure that each school-aged child has his/her own calendar. Special family outings, church activities, doctor's appointments, and even the kids' tests can be recorded on calendars. This has sure helped communication in our family!

I have recently discovered a wonderful planner* that is helping me immensely. From the following sample pages 62 and 63, you can see how it simplifies the daily juggling act of a working mom.

Here are some ideas that you may want to include on your calendar:

- If you are married, don't forget to schedule regular time with your mate. When our sons were smaller, Jim and I would make it a practice to spend the first ten to fifteen minutes of the evening together, just visiting about the day. The boys knew that this was "our time." And remember to schedule regular date nights together. A strong marriage gives kids security and roots.
- If you are a single working mom, hopefully your children spend quality time with their dad. If not, seek out a positive male role model from your family, church, or neighborhood.

---

* Planner pads can be ordered from Planner Pads® Co., P.O. Box 27187, Omaha, NE 68127-0187, 402-592-0676.

- Whether married or single, schedule time for yourself—for personal Bible studies and to just unwind.
- Take turns planning family nights. Let the kids choose if they want to play a board game, go bowling, go on a picnic, or just read books by a blazing fire.
- Plan the errands that you must run during the day. Anticipate the path that you travel to and from work, and try to incorporate as much as possible into one trip. This will give you more time to be with those you love.
- When possible, utilize your lunch hours to lighten your load at home. I know one woman who spends her lunch hour cleaning her house.
- As your kids get older, it will become important to determine which family activities are negotiable and which are not. Our family takes a vacation together every year and this is not negotiable. (We've found that this time not only gives us rest and relaxation, but gives us special time to focus on one another, without interruptions and schedules.) Going to church on Sundays is not negotiable, nor is being home by curfew. However, the time for dinner, selection of activities, and clothing choices (within reason) are negotiable. And as the boys entered their late teens, they were also free to visit other churches besides the one Jim and I call "home."
- A friend of mine, Anje Anstaett, is a busy mom who homeschools her children. She gives each of her children a bulleted list of various chores and school tasks based on their ages and abilities. The children color the bullets when they

PLANNING FOR THE WEEK OF: May 12 - 18

WEEKLY LISTS OF ACTIVITIES BY CATEGORIES

Church	School	Booster Club	Talent Show
✓ Call re. Youth Trip	✓ Field Trip Form	✓ Call re. vol.	✓ Schedule tryouts
✓ Get book for	✓ Picture money	for concession	✓ Send participants
✓ Bible Study	✓ Find someone	stands	lts with
✓ moms mtg.	for Wed's	✓ Order t-shirts	details
	Carpool - Sue		
	✓ Schedule mtg		
	with Mrs Jones		
	Thurs.		

DAILY THINGS-TO-DO

MONDAY 12	TUESDAY 13	WEDNESDAY 14	THURSDAY 15
✓ Call re concessions	✓ Schedule mtg	✓ Send field trip	Order T-shirts
" " Youth Group	with Mrs Jones	forms to	
✓ Get bk for	✓ Call concession	school	
Bible study	stand vol.	with picture	
✓ Call Sue re	✓ ask Mrs Jones		
Carpool	re Tal. Show		
finish article	tryouts		
on family	✓ Send Martin's		
	materials		

APPOINTMENTS

	MONDAY		TUESDAY		WEDNESDAY		THURSDAY
7:		7:		7:		7:	
8:		8:		8:30 ⎫		8:	
9:		9:	Computer Class	9: ⎬ Staff mtg		9:	Mrs Jones
10:		10:		10: ⎭		10:	
11:		11:		11:		11:	
12:		12:		12:		12:	
1:		1:		1:		1:	
2:	Dept mtg	2:30	Carpool	2:00 ⎫ meet with		2:30	Carpool
3:		3:		3:30 ⎭ Julie		3:	
4:		4:		4:		4:	
5:		5:		5:		5:	
6:		6:		6:00 Church		6: ⎫ FAMILY	
7:		7:00	Bible Study	7:		7: ⎬ NIGHT	
8:		8:		8:		8:	
9:		9:		9:		9: ⎭	

PLANNER PAD®

62

MAJOR GOAL THIS WEEK:

WEEKLY LISTS OF ACTIVITIES BY CATEGORIES

NOTES/CALLS

Work	Letters to Write	Music
✓ Finish Article	✓ Mom	Birthday Card for Lynn
Send Joe & Sue	Cy & Evelyn	
Martin Conference	T-Y Parkers	
materials		
✓ Take Computer Class		

Concessions
Fri —
Be there
at 6 P.M.

Pastor Smith —
228-1234
(Youth trip)
Baptist Book Store —
225-3333
Sue (re carpool) —
664-5858
Becky - 228-9347
Nan - 568-6584
Bob - 224-5298
Kate - 661-9942

T-Shirt Shop —
372-4242
School - 868-1111

DAILY THINGS-TO-DO

FRIDAY 16	SATURDAY 17	SUNDAY 18
	Clean house	
	dog to vet	

EXPENSES

ARMED FORCES DAY

APPOINTMENTS

FRIDAY	SATURDAY	SUNDAY	
6: Be at Concession Stands			Groceries:
7:	7:	7:	peppers
8: Baseball Game	8:	8:	shampoo
9:	9:	9:15 Sunday School	paper towels
10:	10:	10:45 Church	
11:	11:	11:	
12:	12:	12: mom's for	
1: moms mtg.	1:	1: lunch	
2:	2:	2:	
3:	3:	3:	
4:	4:	4:	
5:	5:	5:	
6:	6:	6: Church	
7:	7: Date with	7:	
8:	8: Jim	8:	
9:	9:	9:	

			MAY			
S	M	T	W	T	F	S
				1	2	3
4	5	6	7	8	9	10
11	12	13	14	15	16	17
18	19	20	21	22	23	24
25	26	27	28	29	30	31

PLANNER PAD®
©

63

complete specific chores and assignments. Here is one list for her eight-year-old daughter Sarah.

- Spend time with God
- Make your bed
- Brush and floss your teeth
- Sort your laundry
- Spelling—pretest 18
- Spelling—pp. 72–73
- Math lessons 54–56
- Italic—p. 30
- Explode the Code—lesson 6
- Dictation
- Help clean your bathroom
- Help fold towels

MEAL AND KITCHEN TIPS

*Better a meal of vegetables where there is love
than a fattened calf with hatred.*

PROVERBS 15:17

- Use baskets and containers in your kitchen. A large plastic storage box is great for holding boxes of cereal.
- Keep a basket in your kitchen for everyone's Bibles.
- Keep an ongoing list of grocery needs on the refrigerator or family bulletin board. Have everyone in the family add items as needed.
- Use frozen loaves of bread found at your local grocery store. This is the easy way to make "homemade" bread.
- Assign cooking nights for the entire family. Younger children can make simple dishes like spaghetti and macaroni and cheese.

- Save those leftovers for soup.
- Have a regular "pizza" night.
- Clean your refrigerator—one shelf at a time. Sometimes the entire task can be a bit overwhelming, so break it down and just clean portions of your refrigerator every day.
- Remember the crock pot!
- Double casseroles—one for dinner and the other for either the freezer or friends.
- Make a family recipe book (complete with special memories of various recipes).
- Keep it simple. If your family likes a spaghetti sauce mix, use it and save yourself valuable time.

CLOTHES

Consider how the lilies grow. They do not labor or spin.
Yet I tell you, not even Solomon in all his splendor
was dressed like one of these.

LUKE 12:27

- Go through the closets regularly and give away items that have not been worn for a year. (OK, OK, I have not done this myself. But it really is a good idea!)
- Keep a few garbage sacks in the trunk of the car. They are great after muddy soccer games. Just have your child step into the sack and—presto—the dirt stays in the sack and not on the car.
- Have the kids choose what they are going to wear to school the night before. You may want to have a chair that is designated for all of the clothing items that will be needed in the morn-

ing. This will be especially helpful for a daughter's choice of hair bows, socks, and necklaces.

- Keep a shoe rack by the back door (hopefully in the garage or in a side room). Use it for muddy shoes and football cleats.
- Give young kids choices—"Would you rather wear this or that tomorrow?" Handle clothing choices before they become issues.
- Keep a few sweaters and light jackets in the trunk of your car if you frequently attend sporting events.
- Put a clothes hamper by the back door for all of those smelly, dirty practice uniforms and P.E. clothes.
- You may want to give your children different colored baskets to help with sorting laundry. One example would be white clothes going into a white basket, colored clothes into a red basket, and blue clothes into a blue basket. (A friend of mine actually has her four kids sort clothes into six baskets: whites, denim jeans, dark clothes, light colored clothes [not woven], light colored clothes [woven], and towels.)
- It really helps if you can spread out your wash and not have to do it all on one day.

HOUSEWORK

Whatever you do, work at it with all your heart,
as working for the Lord, not for men.

COLOSSIANS 3:23

- Set a timer and have everyone do their assigned chores. When the timer goes off, everyone gets ice cream or pizza.

- Write various chores on pieces of paper and have a weekly "drawing for chores."
- Keep an ongoing list of repair projects around the house.
- Evaluate your storage space. Once I had old college yearbooks taking up prime storage space. They have since been moved to the top of a closet.
- Box items that you do not need and put them in the attic or basement. Be sure and put a list of contents in the lid of the box and keep a copy of this in a notebook elsewhere.
- Use a basket for the TV remote so it won't continually get "lost."
- Reward yourself and periodically hire someone to clean your house.
- Discuss as a family how teamwork helps lighten chores (picking up one's clothes, making up beds, etc.).
- Define a clean room/clean kitchen. (Believe me, the kids' definition will not be yours.)
- Assign specific areas of your home to each child/adult which they will keep clean. (Example: one child may be responsible for the den, another the kitchen, Dad may keep the garage clean, and Mom might regularly clean the bathrooms. Of course, assignments can vary from week to week.)
- And don't forget regular household duties—kids can help with loading and unloading the dishwasher, setting the table, taking out the trash, making the beds, etc. You are actually training children for lifelong habits. (Their future spouse will appreciate this!)

School Tips

Teach me to do your will, for you are my God;
may your good Spirit lead me on level ground.

PSALM 143:10

- Have one centralized place where book bags, lunches, permission sheets, etc., are placed.
- Give your children emergency change for unplanned phone calls.
- Keep library books in one place.
- Jot down the number of library books that you have checked out and their due dates. I do this on the family calendar. (Example: Chris-3; John-5; Mary-1; this has helped me determine if I have all of the books when it is time to return them.)
- Remember to look at notices from school and jot down school events on the family calendar.

Communication Tips

Hear this, all you peoples; listen, all who live in this world,
both low and high, rich and poor alike.

PSALM 49:1–2

- Keep spiral notebooks by all phones to record (and date) phone messages.
- If you work on a kitchen or dining room table, gather your papers/crafts and put them in a storage box that fits under a bed. Your materials will still be accessible and the table will stay neater when you are not working on it.
- Keep a small notebook that has dividers for home/work/prayer requests. Slip a plastic zippered sleeve in this notebook for pens/stamps/note cards.

- Keep a large spiral notebook with dividers. Have sections for various church/school/sports activities. This is where you can keep team rosters, phone lists, committee lists, etc. This has helped me time and time again!
- Have good news/bad news time at the dinner table. (Everyone tells the best and worst things that happened that day.)
- Model integrity. For example, if you are not charged for something at the store, bring this to the clerk's attention and be sure your child realizes the importance of honesty.
- Pull out the family calendar when you are going through the mail. Record dates immediately.
- Keep a supply of greeting cards, thank-you notes, and stationery on hand. Keep some in the car, too, so you can maximize time spent in the car.

ENTERTAINING THE KIDS

When I was a child, I talked like a child,
I thought like a child, I reasoned like a child.

1 CORINTHIANS 13:11

- Have a kitchen cabinet with plastic bowls and pans for small children to play with.
- Cut out a picture from a magazine and glue some cardboard to the back of it. Then cut the picture into pieces to make a puzzle.
- Tape record your favorite Bible stories and Scriptures for your children.
- Use an egg timer to show that "Mom is having her special time."
- Keep a neighbor's kids and vice versa.

- Have a box of "junk" that kids can use to make things while you are having your quiet time.
- Begin reading a story to your children and let them end it.
- Make up stories with your surroundings.
- Have special things for children to do in a plastic storage box (coloring books, reading books, etc.). Keep this in the car for long trips or various sporting events.

MISCELLANEOUS

*May he give you the desire of your heart
and make all your plans succeed.*

PSALM 20:4

- Keep one or two sets of guest linens in your closet (include sheets and towels) in a plastic zippered bag. (This way, you will always have clean linens for guests.)
- Have an outside bell mounted on your house to ring for your kids when you want them to come home.
- Give your kids the responsibility of feeding pets (use a pet feeder when you go out of town).
- Fill a kitchen drawer with play dough, puzzles, plastic bowls, etc., for little ones to play with while you are busy with meals or on the phone.

* * *

As working moms, we truly realize that time is limited. So much so that even the lunch hour means far more than food to us. We may be found throwing a load of clothes in the washer, vacuuming our homes, starting supper in a crock pot, or running errands.

Although God only gives us twenty-four hours in a day, may we be women who maximize our time at home—after all, it is the place where life happens with those we love.

SCRIPTURE FOR REFLECTION

I will instruct you and teach you in the way you should go;
I will counsel you and watch over you.

PSALM 32:8

If the Lord delights in a man's way,
he makes his steps firm;
though he stumble, he will not fall,
for the Lord upholds him with his hand.

PSALM 37:23–24

Whatever you do, work at it with all your heart,
as working for the Lord, not for men, since you know that
you will receive an inheritance from the Lord as a reward.
It is the Lord Christ you are serving.

COLOSSIANS 3:23–24

QUESTIONS TO PONDER

1. Where am I succeeding with the limited time that God gives me?

2. What are some areas in my life that could use a little organization?

3. During what times have I acted like a martyr—as though I have to do everything myself?

4. How can members of my family help me accomplish various tasks at home? (You will have to discuss this question with your family.)

CHAPTER 5

WHERE'S MY TREASURE?

Make sure the thing you are living for is worth dying for.

CHARLES MAYES

Several years ago, Jim and I went on a vacation with the boys to Missouri, where we visited Ha Ha Tonka State Park. As we drove up one particularly steep mountain by the Lake of the Ozarks, we could see a huge structure in the distance. But as we approached it, we realized that it was just a shell—the ruins of what had surely been a magnificent castle. We talked about what we thought had happened, and finally imagined that pirates attacked it long ago, leaving behind just a reminder of what once had been a masterpiece.

When we reached the site of the remains, there stood a large sign telling its history. We learned that the stone ruins were all that was left of one man's dream. In the early 1900s, Robert McClure Snyder, a prominent Kansas businessman, had envisioned a private retreat, the center of which was to be a European-style castle. The fortress was designed with sixty rooms that were grouped on three floors around a central hall that rose three and a half stories to a skylight. Nine greenhouses, a stone carriage house, and an eighty-foot-high water tower were built near the main structure.

After only one year of construction, Snyder was killed in an automobile accident in 1906. The castle's interior was finally completed by his son in 1922, but sparks from a fireplace began a tragic fire in 1942 that gutted both the castle and carriage house.

When I read about Snyder's mansion, strange as it may seem, I thought, *What do I want my legacy to be? A gorgeous palace? A beautiful garden? Perhaps a painting that would be considered a masterpiece?*

I was reminded of Matthew 6:19–21: "Do not store up for yourselves treasures on earth, where moth and rust destroy, and where thieves break in and steal. But store up for yourselves treasures in heaven, where moth and rust do not destroy, and where thieves do not break in and steal. For where your treasure is, there your heart will be also."

Rather than a legacy of possessions or fame, I want to raise godly children. As the castle ruins at Ha Ha Tonka State Park so visually portrayed, things can be destroyed in a moment. But values, character, and a Christian heritage can be passed on from one generation to the next.

SERVING THE LORD AT WORK AND HOME

Mom, where is your treasure? Do you realize that God could be using you, this very day, to make an impact on the world as you raise the next generation? Be revitalized by these words:

I learned more about Christianity from my mother than from all the theologians of England.—John Wesley (John Blanchard, *Gathering Gold*, 103)

The best time to tackle a minor problem is before he grows up.—Anonymous (John Blanchard, *Gathering Gold*, 101)

My mother was the most beautiful woman I ever saw. All I am I owe to my mother. I attribute all my success in life to the moral, intellectual, and physical education I received from her.—George Washington (*Mothers: A Tribute*, 38)

All that I am or hope to be I owe to my angel mother. I remember my mother's prayers and they have always followed me. They have clung to me all my life.—Abraham Lincoln (*Mothers: A Tribute*, 36)

Never think of yourself as "just a wife and mom." You're a molder of leaders, a gatekeeper of peace, a channel through which God's Word can be instilled into the next generation. Quite an overwhelming charge, isn't it? But don't be dismayed.

When we find ourselves working much of the day, exactly how can we serve the Lord at work and home—fulfilling his plan and purpose for our lives? I am reminded of Paul's words in 2 Corinthians 12:9–10: "But he said to me, 'My grace is sufficient for you, for my power is made perfect in weakness.' Therefore I will boast all the more gladly about my weaknesses, so that Christ's power may rest on me. That is why, for Christ's sake, I delight in weaknesses, in insults, in hardships, in persecutions, in difficulties. For when I am weak, then I am strong."

And I think that God whispers in an especially loving voice to working moms, "My grace is sufficient for you, for my power is made perfect when you are tired—but have much to do for those you love."

Whether we are at home or at work, we need the Holy Spirit's help to be godly mothers and employees. We can only do this by spending time alone with God—in his Word—and obeying what we learn as he teaches.

Mom, when you and I feel the stress of balancing home and work responsibilities, we must look to God. He is waiting for us when waters are deep. He is indeed awesome and able. After all, he is our sovereign God, the potter molding the clay as he desires.

Yet, despite the knowledge of God's provisions for me— and my heart for my family—sometimes I have found myself getting caught up in the events of work And there are those times when I have felt totally discouraged. It is then that the Almighty God, the Creator of this entire universe seems to gently tap me on the shoulder and say, "Mary, remember your priorities—God, family, and then work." At these times I have to examine my motives. Do I want to glorify God or myself?

Several years ago I read Steven Covey's book, *The Seven Habits of Highly Effective People.* In it he suggests that individuals write a personal creed. I wrote, "Love God with all my heart. Allow Christ to live through me as I love God, Jim, our children, myself, and others. Do whatever work God entrusts to me with excellence and unto the Lord—not man."

Whenever I review my "creed," it reminds me that I was bought with a high price and that God has special plans for my life. God is sovereign, no matter what the situation might be. I have to keep reminding myself, "Do whatever work God entrusts to me with excellence and *unto the Lord*—not man."

I often ask, "Am I allowing Christ to really live through me when I act a certain way? Do I want credit for myself or do I want to give all of the honor to God? Am I striving for excellence to glorify the Lord, or just to please my boss? Does a certain matter really make all that much difference in light of eternity?"

If you have not already worked through Henry Blackaby's and Claude King's book, *Experiencing God,* I highly suggest that you do this. Their major premise is that God is at work around us and that he invites us to join him in his work. It has been exciting and encouraging to give my life over to Christ and see what work he wants to accomplish through me. After all, he is already at work around you and me, we need only to join him and truly experience his presence and purpose. He is the Master and has the master plan for our lives.

WE MUST PUT ON THE ARMOR OF GOD

Our son John participated in a speech contest when he was about eleven years old. His topic was "The Armor of God." Allow me to share his words with you:

> You must put on the full armor of God if you are to live a godly life and be protected from Satan's temptations. You need to be filled with the Lord and fight the battle against the devil. You may wonder what the armor of God is.
>
> The Bible tells that the armor of God is the belt of truth, the breastplate of righteousness, the shoes of the gospel of peace, the shield of faith, and most importantly the sword of the spirit, which is the Word of God. As it says in Ephesians 6:10–12: "You must be strong in the Lord and in his mighty power. You should put on the full armor of God so that you may take your stand against the devil's schemes."
>
> You must walk in truth and stay away from the sins of deceitfulness. In Ephesians 6:16 it tells us that

you must take up the shield of faith so that you can extinguish all of the fiery darts of the evil one. This means that you need to have faith to be able to take a stand against all of Satan's lies and temptations and tricks that may fool us. Jesus was tempted by Satan when he went out into the desert. Satan tempted Jesus by telling him to turn a rock into some bread since he was very hungry. But Jesus didn't listen to Satan. He just quoted Scripture and told the devil that man cannot live by bread alone. We cannot listen to Satan. The armor of God is like the armor that a warrior puts on before battle. If he doesn't wear the armor, he will get killed.

It is the same way with God's armor. If we can't put it on we will be led away from the Lord. Many of Satan's tricks have fooled us, like thinking that you need to have many possessions and that you need to be "cool" or popular. Having lots of clothes and shoes cannot help us any in life because they are just pleasures. Many people don't think of these things as tricks but just that they are things they need.

You can't just wear the Lord's armor when you need it most; you must wear it all of the time. Satan may sneak up on you and catch you off guard when you are tired and weary, or even when you are in a good mood. You need to always be prepared for anything at any time. By yourself you cannot withstand the devil's tricks; you must have the Lord's help and you need to pray daily on all occasions with all kinds of prayers and requests. You need to keep this in mind and always keep on praying for everybody. You need to be strong in the Lord, and with his mighty power. You must put on the full armor of God!

You know, I think John really captured the secret to successful living in his essay. We must put on the armor of God. When we don't, why are we surprised when Satan's attacks are so successful? (Now that John will soon be in college, I think it is time for me to dust off the pages of his sixth-grade essay and share it with him. He had some good advice that is still very true for his life and mine today.)

ENCOURAGE YOURSELF WITH THE WORD OF GOD

It has really helped me at work to keep a list of encouraging Bible verses on my computer. (Of course, you can always record these in a notebook if you do not have access to a computer.) Many times I have referred to these verses and given them to others. Just begin with one verse, and add others as the Lord leads you. The following list includes some of my favorite verses:

Topic	Reference	Verse
Rest in the Lord	Exodus 14:14	"The LORD will fight for you; you need only to be still."
Sovereignty	Habakkuk 2:20	"But the LORD is in his holy temple; let all the earth be silent before him."
Protection	Proverbs 2:8	"For he guards the course of the just and protects the way of his faithful ones."
Praise	Psalm 115:1	"Not to us, O LORD, not to us but to your name be the glory, because of your love and faithfulness."

Faithfulness	Genesis 5:24	"Enoch walked with God."
Trust	Proverbs 16:20	" . . . Blessed is he who trusts in the LORD."
Sovereignty	Psalm 139:12	"Even the darkness is not dark to Thee" (NASB).
Lord's presence	Psalm 42:8	"The LORD will command his loving-kindness in the daytime; And his song will be with me in the night" (NASB).
Instruction	Psalm 25:8	"Good and upright is the LORD; therefore he instructs sinners in his ways."
Trust	Deut. 31:6	"Be strong and courageous. Do not be afraid or terrified because of them, for the LORD your God goes with you; he will never leave you nor forsake you."
Faithfulness	1 Thess. 5:24	"The one who calls you is faithful and he will do it."
Anxiety	Psalm 94:19	"When my anxious thoughts multiply within me, Thy consolations delight my soul" (NASB).
Hope	Psalm 20:4	"May he give you the desire of your heart and make all your plans succeed."

Trust	2 Chron. 20:20	"Have faith in the LORD your God and you will be upheld; have faith in his prophets and you will be successful."
Purpose	Psalm 119:73–74	"Your hands made me and formed me; give me understanding to learn your commands. May those who fear you rejoice when they see me, for I have put my hope in your word."
Hope	2 Sam. 22:29	"You are my lamp, O LORD; the LORD turns my darkness into light. With your help I can advance against a troop; with my God I can scale a wall."

I cannot begin to tell you how God has rejuvenated me time and time again through these, and other, Bible verses. Just think of it, Mom, when your plate is about to topple over: God will fight for you, even when it is pitch black—darker than the innermost part of a cave. Yes, even then it is not dark to God!

Oh, how wonderful it is when, like Enoch, I walk with God. And it is really my choice. God is there all of the time— he is faithful, consoling, a light to my path. He only asks that I take his hand through his Word and prayer, and put on the armor of God.

"So, exactly how does one serve the Lord at home and work?" you ask. Do you recall the story of the lumberjack that I shared earlier in this book? He did not take the time to sharpen his ax. As working moms, we must get the physical rest that our bodies need and also be in God's Word regularly. For only then can the Master lead us—and his song will be with us, even in the midst of whatever seems like night. What a promise! What a hope!

As God said to King Jehoshaphat in 2 Chronicles 20:15, "This is what the LORD says to you: 'Do not be afraid or discouraged because of this vast army. For the battle is not yours, but God's.'" I can give even my smallest daily battle at home or work to the Lord, and he will direct me as I walk with him. But I sure can get myself in trouble when I forget this and act as though I am in control of the battle plan apart from God's direction. Logic cannot be trusted. Feelings cannot be trusted. But the Word of God and his faithfulness will never fail us. Never.

GOD IS IN CONTROL

And Mom, we must rest in the fact that no matter what circumstances we are walking in, God is sovereign. ("God's sovereignty is his exercise of rule [as 'sovereign' or 'king'] over his creation" (Wayne Grudem, *Systematic Theology* [Grand Rapids: Zondervan Publishing House, 1994], 217). Although Job understood this, his wife did not. Job 2:9–10 tells us that Job's wife said to him, "'Are you still holding on to your integrity? Curse God and die!' He replied, 'You are talking like a foolish woman. Shall we accept good from God, and not trouble?'" And in Job 42:2, Job says to God, "I know that you can do all things; no plan of yours can be thwarted."

Although you and I make choices that do have definite consequences, we are not in ultimate control. God is. Over the years, I have gathered various articles that reminded me of God's sovereignty. I'd like to share a few excerpts with you:

"A Navy F-14 fighter jet heavy with fuel crashed in a fiery explosion in a neighborhood Monday, demolishing three houses and killing five people" (*Arkansas Democrat-Gazette,*

January 30, 1996, 1A). Why those five people? I imagine that some of them may have come home after a hard day at work, looking forward to a night of rest and relaxation in the one place that they knew they could find it—home. Why did God allow this?

And the headlines of the *Arkansas Democrat-Gazette* (our hometown newspaper) on November 16, 1996, read "Shots at rest stop gas station kill 2 traveling in state." This one really struck home because the older gentleman who was killed at the rest stop was the grandfather of one of our son's friends. All this man was trying to do was take a break as he traveled from Illinois to Memphis. How could our good Lord have permitted this?

You may recall the crash of TWA Flight 800 in 1996. Eileen Rence, then fifty-one, was supposed to be on that flight. "But foul weather delayed the first leg of her trip to Chicago's O'Hare Airport by four hours, so she didn't arrive in New York until 7:50 P.M.—10 minutes before the ill-fated TWA flight took off" (*Arkansas Democrat-Gazette,* July 19, 1996, 7A). I imagine when she missed her connection in New York her first reaction was frustration and perhaps even anger at just barely missing her flight. But God allowed a seemingly divine interruption in the life of a middle-aged woman, while allowing even children and young adults to perish in this tragic crash. Why?

What about Alice Hawthorne? She "had heard how beautiful the Atlantic Olympics were from her sister, who was working at the Games. So she and her daughter, who had just turned 14, packed up and went. Early Saturday, the 44-year-old woman was killed when a bomb exploded during a concert in downtown Atlanta's Centennial Olympic Park" (*Arkansas Democrat-Gazette,* July 28, 1996, 9A). Why? Out of all of the millions of people who went to the Olympics, why was this one woman singled out?

Then there is little Joshua Walls. The *Arkansas-Democrat-Gazette* told how "Jim and Sue Walls lost their son and daughter-in-law to a tornado last month, but they are still celebrating a Christmas miracle. Their 7-month-old grandson, Joshua, survived the November 10 tornado that obliterated his home near Des Arc, threw him the length of three football fields and killed his parents . . ." December 25, 1995, 1A). Why? Why did God spare this child in the rage of a killer tornado?

And several years ago a disgruntled, unemployed welder entered the Ohio Bureau of Workers' Compensation with his three young boys and threatened to start a fire. He took three hostages. One of the hostages, "James Carter, had started a job with the agency just three days earlier after working for the FBI for 25 years. Carter, 58, jumped Dailey and officers stormed in" (*Arkansas Democrat-Gazette,* November 15, 1996, 4A). Now, how could this be just a coincidence? How could a former FBI agent just happen to have been taken as a hostage?

Finally, there was the story of a cat calling 911. Yes, you read that right. "Tipper the cat knocked a telephone off the hook while choking on his flea collar and somehow hit the No. 1 on the key pad, which automatically dialed 911. . . . Banforth arrived at the mobile home of Gail Curtis, who was out. Hearing the cat inside, the deputy got the key from the park manager.

"The gray and white tabby was in a corner, the flea collar rolled up in his mouth. The deputy and a maintenance worker quieted the cat and removed the collar. Tipper is now just fine" (*Arkansas Democrat-Gazette,* July 12, 1996, 4A). Why was this cat saved? How in the world did he "dial" 911?

I think the lesson that God continually tries to show me is that he is in control—not me. As Job said in Job 42:2, "I know that you can do all things; no plan of yours can be thwarted." Sometimes, we just don't know why some things happen. And other times, only the passage of months and years will reveal

God's divine purpose. But regardless, we can find comfort in Romans 8:28: "And we know that in all things God works for the good of those who love him, who have been called according to his purpose." The key question is: Are we willing to submit to God's control and trust him to work everything to his glory in the end?

Mom, God can do anything that is according to his will. No matter why you are working, no matter the state of your home situation, whether you are married, widowed, or divorced— God is in control and desires to use your situation for his glory and your good. Too often I know this in my head but do not act on this in my heart.

As the following poem expresses, at times it is so hard to let something go and give it to God:

As children bring their broken toys with tears for us to mend,
I brought my broken dreams to God because he was my friend.
But then instead of leaving him in peace to work alone,
At last I snatched them back and cried,
"How can you be so slow?"
"My child," he said,
"What could I do?
"You never did let go."

UNKNOWN

Are you holding onto anything and not giving it to God? Are you not trusting his plan for you because you lack understanding? Sometimes I have held onto broken dreams. Even the very writing of this book did not become a reality until I gave this desire totally to the Lord—to fulfill in his time and in his way.

Whether we are young or old, married or single, professional or relatively unskilled, may we focus on God's purpose for us as mothers. Although we may be in the midst of changing diapers or releasing teenagers, there is no higher calling than molding and equipping the next generation. May we remember our source of strength and eternal purpose, and may our treasure be a true desire to glorify only the Lord.

Serving God at home and work—impossible! "But with God all things are possible" (Matt. 19:26).

SCRIPTURES FOR REFLECTION

No one can serve two masters.
Either he will hate the one and love the other,
or he will be devoted to the one and despise the other.
You cannot serve both God and Money.

MATTHEW 6:24

Blessed is the man who does not walk in the counsel of the wicked
or stand in the way of sinners or sit in the seat of mockers.
But his delight is in the law of the Lord,
and on his law he meditates day and night.
He is like a tree planted by streams of water,
which yields its fruit in season and whose leaf does not wither.
Whatever he does prospers. Not so the wicked!
They are like chaff that the wind blows away.
Therefore the wicked will not stand in the judgment,
nor sinners in the assembly of the righteous.
For the Lord watches over the way of the righteous,
but the way of the wicked will perish.

PSALM 1

QUESTIONS TO PONDER

1. Write a personal creed or mission statement below.

2. What are two or three ways that I am applying my mission statement to everyday life?

3. How does my sense of mission encourage me?

4. How am I asking God to help me achieve his priorities and purpose through me? How am I cooperating with him?

5. What are some of my actions and decisions that really show that my heart is at home?

6. What do I want my legacy to be? What changes do I need to make in my life for this to happen? (If you are married, discuss these questions with your husband.)

CHAPTER 6

WOULD THE REAL SUPER MOM PLEASE STAND UP?

The glory is not in never failing,
but in rising every time you fall.

CHINESE PROVERB

It's 8:30 P.M. and the kids are asleep. My second load of wash for the evening is in the spin cycle. If I get up twenty minutes early tomorrow, then I can dry the clothes so Chris's uniform will be ready for his 5:15 P.M. baseball game.

The cupcakes are cooling, and I should have time to ice them tomorrow before John goes to school. It's his birthday! And then there's the $2.50 that Chris needs for his field trip tomorrow. I'll have to put it at his place with his permission form.

I've got an extra casserole in the freezer, so that will take care of dinner tomorrow. Maybe Jim can stop by the bakery and

*pick up John's birthday cake; we'll celebrate after Chris's base-
ball game. And then there's . . .*

What's a working mom to do? Let's be candid. We both
know that Super Mom does not exist, but why do we pretend
that she does? Do you feel guilty when you pull out that green
moldy stuff from a bowl of leftovers in the fridge? I sure do.
And what if an unannounced guest drops by and your house
isn't immaculate? If you come to my house, please do not open
the rolltop desk. You could be knocked down from the force
of all those papers crammed into it.

As Christian working moms, we have many roles to play
which may include: wife, mother, full-time or part-time employee, responsible family member, church, school and civic
volunteer . . . the list goes on and on.

Mom, have you ever put unrealistic expectations on yourself? Somehow, I often think that I should always be cheerful,
Christlike, and have extra energy to not only help the kids with
homework but also to meet the needs of our neighbors on a
daily basis. My home should always be spotless and ready for
any unannounced guests. The laundry should be properly put
away. And, of course, there won't be dirty dishes in the sink.
But this is impossible! I just cannot work full-time and have a
perfectly managed home. I really need to remember that my
main priority when at home is being a wife and mom, meeting
the important needs of my family. Someday the kids will be
grown, and the house can then be spotless. But it will also be
very quiet. I need to appreciate the clutter. It must mean that
life is going on.

I can still vividly recall one day when I knew for sure that
I needed to slow down. I was picking up my husband's suit
from the cleaners and was asked for the last four digits of our
home phone number. (That's how clothing is organized at our
particular cleaners.) I remember the sense of mild panic when

I could not remember them. I had drawn a blank. *Couldn't they have asked an easier question?* I thought lightheartedly to myself. Finally the numbers came to me and I went home with the suit. When things like this happen, I know that I am on the competition trail for the unrealistic "Super Mom of the Year" award. I am doing far too much and need to slow down.

And I will never forget the day when I started the coffeemaker (at work, no less) and forgot to put the coffeepot on the warmer. What a mess! But do you know what? I discovered a great spot remover that even takes out coffee stains from carpets.

I think of a young friend of mine who has a baby and is employed full-time. Her husband not only works full-time, but also is finishing his college degree. He gets very angry if she does not keep a perfect house and have a home-cooked meal prepared every night. Mom, you and I know that these are unrealistic expectations. Could even we, as Christians, find ourselves competing for the "Super Family" award and miss the prize that Christ has in store for us?

I really like what Jean Fleming says in *A Mother's Heart* (Colorado Springs: Navpress, 1996, p. 53): "A sentence from Psalm 101 has been both challenging and convicting for me: 'I will walk in my house with blameless heart'. When God speaks to me about being more loving, this verse reminds me to make application in my family first—and then to others. It forces me to ask, 'Am I more spiritual, more loving, or more fun somewhere else? Who gets my best—my family or others?'"

GOD'S VERSION OF SUPER MOM

It seems in the world's economy that Super Mom does exist and can do and have it all. But what is God's definition of "all"? His Super Mom walks with a blameless heart in her home. She models biblical values through her daily actions. Let's look again at Proverbs 31. What traits describe this remarkable woman?

Noble character (v. 10)

Worthy of husband's confidence (v. 11)

Valuable (vv. 10–11)

Brings her husband only good (v. 12)

Delegates (v. 15)

Hard worker (vv. 13–19, 22, 24, 27)

Helps the poor and needy (v. 20)

Plans well for the unforeseen (v. 21)

Clothed with strength and dignity (v. 25)

Her words are wise (v. 26)

She teaches others (v. 26)

She focuses on her household (v. 27)

Her children and husband respect and honor her (v. 28)

She fears the Lord (v. 30)

Webster's New World Dictionary defines noble as "(1) having or showing a very good character or high morals; lofty; (2) of or having a high rank or title; (3) grand; splendid." The Proverbs 31 woman's husband could trust her completely because of her spiritual nobility. And we see in verse 31 that she receives not only accolades from her family, but also at the city gate. Her concern for her own family and hard work are highly honored. So much so that verse 10 tells us that she is worth far more than rubies.

She brings her husband only good (v. 12). I confess, I have not always done this. There have been times when I have been especially tired after a long day of home and work responsibilities, and I have not spoken or acted kindly to Jim. Yet 1 Peter 3:1–2 says: "Wives, in the same way be submissive to your husbands so that, if any of them do not believe the word, they may be won over without words by the behavior of their wives, when they see the purity and reverence of your lives."

God's perfect desire is that wives would bring their husbands only good. (Whether we are married or single, our entire lives should point people to Christ.)

The Proverbs 31 woman was a hard worker. As a working mom, I think, *Well, I certainly work hard—very hard.* But what describes her work? She toils eagerly and vigorously—at times into the night (vv. 13, 17–18). Although her main concern is her family, she reaches out to others as she helps those in need (v. 20). Her life is not self-consumed. Since she speaks with wisdom, I believe she knew truth—which is found in God's Word. Verse 29, "Many women do noble things, but you surpass them all," tells me that she is honored not for what she does, but rather for who she is. Her fear of the Lord and obedience to his desires resulted in a woman with the right priorities.

Mom, this speaks to me. With discipline, I think virtually anyone can work hard. But what is a Christian mom's goal of this hard work? Are we choosing proper priorities and spending our time as God desires? How does God's Word individually speak to us concerning working outside the home, schooling issues, and time at home with our children? Scripture does tell us that we should honor and respect our husband, manage our homes well, and live in such a way that our children will recognize that our strength comes from the Lord.

SEEK THE LORD

As Christians, we should seek God's will for our lives through prayer and time in his Word. We are told "The Spirit searches all things, even the deep things of God" (1 Cor. 2:10), and "The man without the Spirit does not accept the things that come from the Spirit of God, for they are foolishness to him, and he cannot understand them, because they are spiritually discerned" (1 Cor. 2:14). The Holy Spirit will lead and direct us as we discern God's will for our families. We must not condemn ourselves because of what others may say.

I have been in settings where it was implied that a woman was not a good mother if she worked outside the home. And I have heard others insinuate that a woman is not fulfilled if she "just stays at home." I know people whose divorce was based on biblical grounds, and yet they have heavy hearts when people have seemed to look down upon them because of their marital status.

Mom, you and I are not God—and neither are those around us. Our goal is to please the Lord and rest in knowing that he does not judge according to external appearances (Gal. 2:6). In Luke 16:15 Jesus himself told the Pharisees, "You are the ones who justify yourselves in the eyes of men, but God knows your hearts." And if God knows our hearts, then I believe he will help and direct us, as Christians who seek to please and obey him. Depending upon our circumstances, this may lead some to become stay-at-home moms, others to work part-time or change jobs, and still others to continue working outside the home just as they are currently doing.

Search the Scriptures, pray, and ask the Lord to show you his wisdom for your life. We are promised in James 1:5: "If any of you lacks wisdom, he should ask God, who gives generously to all without finding fault, and it will be given to him." That's exactly what the Proverbs 31 woman did—she feared the Lord and obediently followed his direction for her life.

It tells us in Proverbs 31:15 that this unique woman had servants. She undoubtedly delegated responsibilities, and we working moms must do likewise. In order for us to redeem some time, I think it is vital that we enlist the help of our family members and also network with friends and neighbors. And if you are married, enlist your husband's help. (You may need to explain that "doing the dishes" is not just moving them from the table to the sink.) Of course, in chapter 4 we went into great detail about how the kids can pitch in and help around the house. You may even need to hire someone to clean your home periodically so you can spend more time with your family. Jim and I did this when our children were younger.

STRIVE FOR BALANCE

I think a godly mom who works needs to have balance as one of her desires. She realizes that God and her family are her first priorities, and also admits her limitations. She realizes that she cannot be all things to all people at all times. Proverbs 2:6, 9 tells us that we must call out to God for understanding and insight: "For the Lord gives wisdom, and from his mouth come knowledge and understanding. . . . Then you will understand what is right and just and fair—every good path."

You may want to ask your husband's help in determining proper priorities. Jim is a wonderful sounding board for me. I have found that I am often too quick to volunteer, so I try to ask his advice before I commit to something that will take time away from our family. (Jim seems to know my limits better than I do.) If you are not married, I suggest that you have a female friend who will be your accountability partner. Ask her for advice when it comes to adding more to your juggling act. Where must you win? Yes, we can rewind the clock to clean, paint, work, and even volunteer. But we cannot recapture time with our children and somehow shrink them from twenty-year-olds into toddlers. They are only children once.

An ancient Chinese proverb says:

If you are planning for one year, grow rice.
If you are planning for twenty years, grow trees.
If you are planning for centuries, grow men.

I think the Proverbs 31 woman was growing godly men and that her investment into the next generation was seen by not only her husband, but also by those who sat at the city gate. The fear of the Lord was the foundation for her achievements.

If I were to imagine the wording for an advertisement for a mother similar to the one in Proverbs 31, it would say something like this:

Needed: Key individual who wants to impact the world.
Qualifications: Fears the Lord and seeks his wisdom, loyal, dedicated, hard worker, thoughtful, strategic planner, teacher, visionary, respected by her family and community.
Salary: Incalculable—Priceless.
Hours: Entire life.
Benefits: Eternal.
Starting Date: Immediately.

How our country and world need genuine Super Moms: Moms whose goal is to please the Lord, honor and respect their husbands, and train their children in God's ways. Moms who get their direction from God's Word and not from the evening news. Moms whose primary purpose is not to sell houses, teach in schools, type letters, balance corporate budgets, or write books. Moms whose hearts are at home—who fear the Lord and are in the business of growing godly men. May you and I be such women.

SCRIPTURES FOR REFLECTION

There is a time for everything,
and a season for every activity under heaven.

ECCLESIASTES 3:1

"Martha, Martha," the Lord answered,
"you are worried and upset about many things,
but only one thing is needed. Mary has chosen what is better,
and it will not be taken away from her."

LUKE 10:41–42

*Let your light shine before men, that they may see your good
deeds and praise your Father in heaven.*

MATTHEW 5:16

Whatever you do, do it all for the glory of God.

1 CORINTHIANS 10:31

QUESTIONS TO PONDER

1. Read Luke 10:38–42. Why did Christ say that Mary
had chosen what is better?

2. What are my goals for today? For this week? For this
year?

.

3. Why are or aren't my goals realistic? Why do or don't
they match God's desires for me? (If you are married,
discuss this with your spouse.)

CHAPTER 7

HOW DO I INSTILL BIBLICAL VALUES IN MY CHILDREN WITH LIMITED TIME?

I remember my mother's prayers
and they have always followed me.
They have clung to me all my life.

ABRAHAM LINCOLN

As a working mom, do you ever wonder if you are somehow shortchanging your children's spiritual growth by outside employment? I do. But I also know that there are many stay-at-home moms whose kids do not turn out right. Is God capable of fulfilling my desire for a godly home? Of course he is!

As it says in Psalm 31:14–15a, "I trust in you, O LORD; I say, 'You are my God.' My times are in your hands." Not only my days and hours, but also my boys, are in the Lord's hands—this is very comforting.

Jim and I have not done everything right with Chris and John. And if we could turn back the pages of time, we definitely would have done some things differently. But despite our many mistakes, God is working in the lives of our children. Our oldest son has now entered his twenties, and I asked him to share his perspective on being raised in a home where both mom and dad worked. Chris wrote:

I believe raising a family is one of the most important responsibilities God gives parents. However, in a day and time when not all mothers can stay home with their children, there are constant outside threats to raising them under God's principles. Day-care centers, non-Christian instructors and children, and just being away from Mom's guiding hand can be a troublesome thought for any Christian mom to swallow! But I am here to tell you that it can be done! Your child can "taste and see that the Lord is good!" (Ps. 34:8). My life is proof of that.

I am now twenty years old and in college, but my mom has worked even from my earliest memories. Yes, I went to a day-care center, had non-Christian children and teachers around me, and even now attend a secular college. Yet I still love the Lord with all my heart, soul, and might.

There are several things I have learned through growing up with a Christian working mom, and I would like to share them with you. This first point may sound "churchy"—perhaps seem elementary to you—but it is critically important to remember. Use the time you have with your child to teach godly principles and values that he or she will need when facing this "crooked and perverse" generation. Secondly, make family time a special time, and last, make sure lines of communication between you and your child are very open.

In Psalm 119:9 the psalmist said, "How can a young man keep his way pure? By living according to your word." And that is exactly how your child will keep his or her way pure. He must learn to love and live by God's Word. As we all know, children follow Mom and Dad's example, and if you don't live by the Scripture, then why should your children? It is imperative that children see their mom's and dad's lives being led by God through his Word.

Children need to understand that when a decision is made (whether it is choosing a movie to watch or a disciplinary action), that decision is based on the character of God. A particular movie may not be good to see because it puts impure thoughts into our heads (Phil. 4:8), and God is pure. The child may need to be disciplined, not out of anger or hatred, but because God is loving and just (Exod. 20:12). These are a couple of principles that I grew up with.

Praying before every meal and attending church every Sunday was not out of a legalistic idea of "because we have to," but out of love for our Creator and Savior who is worthy of our praise. It was that type of example from my mom and dad that helped me face this world, where man spits in the face of God and exalts himself. Now, I did not have a perfect life and didn't always know what to do when issued a challenge from a non-Christian friend! But it was at those times, when I dug deeper into God's Word, that my faith was strengthened as I discovered why I believed what I did. As children grow up, it will be those strong, biblical roots that hold them steady and tall when the winds of this world try to blow them down (2 Tim. 3:16–17).

The second thing I have learned from growing up with a working mother is that it is important to make family time a special time. Kids need to see that their parents are real people and can be "cool" too, not just seen as the disciplinarian, worker, or couch potato. We have gone on family trips to do some fishing and to see baseball games. We've camped, visited museums, gone shopping, and have done many other "family" activities. And you really don't have to go anywhere to have a special time with your kids! My dad played catch with my brother and me in our yard. Go to the park, play cards or games, or even get a dog.

Think about it! You listen to people you like being around and respect, don't you? It's the same way with your kids. When children see their parents as real people who love the Lord, like to have fun, and admit when they fail, that type of respect comes naturally and they're more prone to value your opinion and listen to your advice. I sure did!

The idea of your child listening to your advice and counsel brings me to my last point: Make sure communication lines with you and your child are open and clear. When you are at work eight hours a day, that is a lot of time to be away! In order to know what went on at school, what he/she did, and what they were taught, you must ask. I vividly remember at dinner every night, my parents would ask what I did during the day. By hearing from John and me, my parents could better understand us and know how to deal with certain situations. Plus, the fact that they asked showed us they cared.

You are the one responsible for your child's education, not some day care, school, or youth center. It is critical that you know what your child is being taught when away from home. If you cannot get an accurate idea from your child, then get a copy of his/her curriculum and review its contents. By addressing issues that run contrary to God's Word, your child will once again have a grasp of biblical principles that he/she needs to know. By being equipped with the Sword of the Spirit, they can effectively combat Satan's attacks on their young minds by knowing whether something is right or wrong. By openly communicating with your children, they will see that you are a friend who cares for them deeply and are interested in everything from school, to friends, to likes and dislikes.

My younger brother and I have been blessed to have two Christian parents. Yes, my mom did work and I know it was a challenge. But God has watched over our family. I have only been around for twenty years, so obviously there are many people wiser than I. That's one thing I love about life and our walk with the Lord: There's always more to learn. But I do believe God has shown me some things that perhaps could help you.

Maybe your family just needs some time together, like a break or vacation. Maybe you should spend more time in meaningful conversation instead of sitting in front of the TV. Perhaps you should get Dad to play catch or go fishing with the kids. Maybe you should look into a Christian day-care center (as many churches provide them) or look at your child's curriculum.

As a product of a Christian family where my mother worked, I can say with boldness and truth: You can raise godly children! Satan will no doubt try to keep you from succeeding at this God-given task, but you can do it. May Proverbs 31:28 ring true to you and may your children "arise and call you blessed."

* * *

Jim and I feel very blessed to have both of our sons, and it is exciting to catch a glimpse of our legacy as we see Chris mature and desire to serve the Lord with his whole heart. Our younger son will soon be graduating from high school and is at a definite fork in the road in his life. There are so many questions concerning his future plans. Someone once said, "I do not know the future, but I do know who holds the future." As Jeremiah 29:11 says, "'I know the plans I have for you,' declares the Lord, 'plans to prosper you and not to harm you, plans to give you hope and a future.'"

Reading Chris's remarks reminds me that God can take imperfect parents, mistakes, sickness, and even tragedies (such as divorce) and fill in the gaps. But no matter what our situations, and no matter how much or little time we have with our children, we must consciously make the effort to instill biblical values in our children. It has also been said that more will be "caught" by our actions than just "taught" by our words.

Jim and I are different people from the two who married almost twenty-five years ago. I was a brand-new Christian. Jim did not accept Christ as his Lord and Savior until Chris was born. We did not know the Bible or what God said about families. But we did know that we wanted a wonderful family and children who loved the Lord. We just needed God's instruction and guidance for doing this.

Our sons, on the other hand, became Christians as little boys and have been in Bible-believing churches their entire lives. As we have grown in the "depths of the riches of the wisdom and knowledge of God" (Rom. 11:33), so have they. Over the years we have hoped to instill biblical values in our children's lives. Perhaps one or two of the following ideas may help your family:

- Every Sunday we share at least one thing that each of us learned during Sunday school and church.

- We pray before meals and at night as a family.
- We took turns being "prayer warriors" when the children were being taken to school. (A "prayer warrior" is just a name for whoever is leading the prayer.)
- We pray in the car before we travel. (We ask God to protect us and then include specific prayer requests such as: that God would open conversations to spiritual matters, that God would help us represent him well as we interact with others, that he would keep the boys free from injury in sporting events, that the car would not have mechanical problems, etc.)
- We have memorized Scripture as a family. Once, the kids took turns teaching a verse to the family at dinnertime, and then wrote it in a spiral notebook.
- At times we have kept logs of prayer requests and God's answers.
- We have tried to model integrity. For example, if we are undercharged, we have let the children know why we returned the excess money.
- We have opened our home up to others. This has been in the form of housing missionaries, tennis players, kids selling books for the summer, and foster children.
- We pray for our sons' future spouses and for their friends. We do this in front of the kids when we pray as a family.
- We discuss decisions in light of God's Word. We have admitted when we did not follow God's Word and had to suffer the consequences. We've discussed with our sons ways in which we would have begun our married life differently.

- We keep a folder called "What we want to teach the boys." In it are various articles, tapes, forms (such as budgeting) that we want to give our sons when they are on their own.
- We have tapes of Bible songs that the kids loved to listen to.
- Jim and I pray and pray and pray for our children.
- The boys were active in AWANA (Approved Workmen Are Not Ashamed)—a Christian club for children that emphasizes Scripture memorization with fun.
- We chose to send our boys to Christian schools through high school.

Other things that we do include praying that all of us will be "caught" if we do something wrong that does not glorify God. And God has been very faithful to answer this prayer. I can picture the day when Jim "happened" to be on the freeway—directly behind a speeding truck that had one of our sons in its bed. A family rule is to never ride in the back of a pickup truck. Jim had quite a discussion with this son, and he has never done this again, and I am sure he never will.

And I clearly remember wanting everything to be perfect for Chris during his first visit home from college—clean house, gourmet meals, goodies for him to take back to school. Yes, we did have a sparkling clean house and delicious food. I even made two of the most beautiful homemade apple pies for Chris to take back to college (with homemade crust, I might add). But all of this came at a high price—our son had a grouchy mother. I had to ask him for forgiveness. In retrospect, it would have been better to have eaten hamburgers in a cluttered house and sent store-bought cookies back to college. I had been "caught." How true are the words of Proverbs 12:18, "Reckless words pierce like a sword, but the tongue of the wise brings healing."

When one of our boys was about ten years old, he returned from a friend's home saying that he needed five dollars. His explanation was that he had been taught to play poker, and he owed someone five dollars. Jim and I were not pleased, and thought that this would be a good time to teach this son about gambling. We told this son (who had no money himself) that he would have to pay his debt and earn the five dollars from someone other than Jim or me. That's actually a lot of money to a young man who's only ten years old.

After knocking on several doors in our neighborhood to see if anyone needed help with chores, he finally found one couple who asked him to mow their yard—on a regular basis, no less. I thought, *How like God.* This son learned a valuable lesson, was able to pay his debt, and was provided a suitable job for his age. What Satan meant for evil, God meant for good (see Gen. 50:20).

As the boys entered high school, they began to make Christian values their own. I recall the words that Joshua said to the Israelites in Joshua 24:14–15, "Now fear the LORD and serve him with all faithfulness. Throw away the gods your forefathers worshiped beyond the River and in Egypt, and serve the LORD. But if serving the LORD seems undesirable to you, then choose for yourselves this day whom you will serve, whether the gods your forefathers served beyond the River, or the gods of the Amorites, in whose land you are living. But as for me and my household, we will serve the LORD." Our sons have the same free will that God gave Joshua and the Israelites—and that he gave you and me. Our children are the ones who have to decide whom they will serve. As parents, we cannot do this for them.

If you have teenagers, you may want to share these "Teen Commandments" with them:

1. Don't let your parents down; they brought you up.
2. Choose your companions with care; you become what they are.
3. Be master of your habits or they'll master you.
4. Treasure your time: don't spend it—invest it.
5. Stand for something or you'll fall for anything.
6. Select a date only with someone who would make a good mate.
7. See what you can do for others, not what they can do for you.
8. Guard your thoughts; what you think, you are.
9. Don't fill up on the world's crumbs; feed your soul on Living Bread.
10. Give your all to Christ; he gave his all for you.

Author Unknown

Parenting is not easy. Actually, godly parenting is downright impossible if we rely upon our own thinking and abilities. When our kids seemed to be at crossroads in their lives, that is when Jim and I would spend special time fasting and praying for them. We knew that a spiritual battle was swirling around them that we could not see. And we were comforted to know that God was on our side. We are told in Romans 8:26–27: "In the same way, the Spirit helps us in our weakness. We do not know what we ought to pray for, but the Spirit himself intercedes for us with groans that words cannot express. And he who searches our hearts knows the mind of the Spirit, because the Spirit intercedes for the saints in accordance with God's will." How comforting to know at those very times when we feel that we are failing as parents, the Holy Spirit is interceding for our family.

Prepare Your Children for Temptation

Mom, don't feel like you are a failure if your kids are being tempted. Satan tempted Jesus Christ himself. We are told in Matthew 4:1: "Then Jesus was led by the Spirit into the desert to be tempted by the devil. After fasting forty days and forty nights, he was hungry. The tempter came to him. . . ." Jesus was tempted at a weak point—he had just fasted for forty days and forty nights. Likewise, Satan will tempt us and our children. Jesus combated Satan's temptations with God's Word. May we learn from the Master's example and turn to Scripture in our time of troubles.

Heed the words of 1 Corinthians 10:12–13: "So, if you think you are standing firm, be careful that you don't fall! No temptation has seized you except what is common to man. And God is faithful; he will not let you be tempted beyond what you can bear. But when you are tempted, he will also provide a way out so that you can stand up under it."

Life today is full of temptation and compromise. That's why we often discuss current events in light of Scripture. You may be asking, "How in the world can someone do that?" Well, not too long ago we talked about the excerpts from a tape transcription that appeared in our local newspaper. One of the parties who was quoted in the excerpt (a federal government employee) said, "I was brought up with lies all the time. . . . That's how you got along. . . . I have lied my entire life. . . ."

If you were to have a discussion about these statements with your children, you might ask them questions such as:

"What do you think about this woman's words? Is it OK to lie? Why do you say this?"

"Why would someone's parents teach them to lie?"

"Are you ever tempted to lie? If so, how can you respond to such temptations?"

"Does it really make a difference to our nation if people lie regularly? Why or why not?"

Then, take out your Bible and as a family look up what God says about lying. You may want to turn to verses such as Psalm 34:13: "Keep your tongue from evil and your lips from speaking lies." John 8:44: "You belong to your father, the devil, . . . for he is a liar and the father of lies." Colossians 3:9: "Do not lie to each other. . . ." Proverbs 6:16: "There are six things the Lord hates, seven that are detestable to him: haughty eyes, a lying tongue, hands that shed innocent blood, a heart that devises wicked schemes, feet that are quick to rush into evil, a false witness who pours out lies, and a man who stirs up dissension among brothers." That's quite a list—and to think that lying is so despicable to God that he mentions it as one of the seven things he absolutely hates!

Now, go back and discuss your original questions with your kids. ("What do you think about this woman's words," etc.) By using God's Word when confronted with daily issues, we show our children the relevance of the Bible and the timelessness of God.

As a child, I remember hearing these words of then Soviet Premier Nikita Khrushchev to the United States: "We will destroy you from within." I was about ten or eleven, and his words truly frightened me. But I have rarely heard a reference to his threat since it was made.

Now, if you and I were to destroy a house from within, how could we do it? I think one of the easiest ways would be to slip a few termites into some wood—perhaps in the walls, attic, or baseboards. If the homeowner chose to simply replace sections of destroyed floors and walls, would he solve his problem? No, he would have to get at the root of the problem and destroy the termites. What are the termites in our world? Could they be our thoughts?

Recently I was in a Bible study where Holly Elliff (wife of Bill Elliff, pastor of Little Rock's First Baptist Church) asked the ladies to brainstorm the names of those who believed things sincerely and deeply, but were wrong. The people mentioned included:

Charles Darwin - Evolution

Adolf Hitler - Murder of Jewish People

Confederacy - Slavery

Karl Marx - Socialism

The list is endless. Centuries ago, people believed that the world was flat. Others once thought that people lived on the moon. Despite how deeply we can believe things, and even act upon such beliefs, it's possible to be wrong, wrong, wrong.

EQUIP YOUR CHILDREN WITH GOD'S WORD

How can we be assured that we are right when it comes to raising our children? We have to destroy the termites in our lives—our improper thoughts. And the only way that we can act on truth is by sifting our thoughts and actions through the Bible. I wish I had begun this at an earlier age.

Psalm 119:105 tells us, "Your word is a lamp to my feet and a light for my path." Imagine that you are walking along a country road one night when there is no moonlight and no stars—only darkness. How comforting it would be if a friend should offer you a lantern—it would light up your path and your feet would not stumble over things you couldn't see.

Well, God offers us perfect light in his Word. The problem is, we are often either too busy to accept his gift, or we just don't believe that it will make a difference in this journey called life. We trip and fall as we travel through time, and then blame God, and ask why he allows certain things to happen. Yet we are the ones who refused his light.

But when we walk in God's light, he will lead us and we will want to praise him. As Ephesians 5:19 says, "Sing and make music in your heart to the Lord." Our sons really enjoy Christian music, and both of them like to compose their own songs.

I realized a few years ago that music has always been important to other generations of our family when I received a letter from my mother: "Thank you for the song. I remember 'I Love to Tell the Story.' That was a favorite and we sang it often. Made me think of when my granddaddy, mother, daddy, Ed, and I went to church. We sat in the same place every Sunday."

After reading that, I thought back to the 1920s when my grandmother and grandfather brought their children to church. Little did they know that the songs they sang would be forever etched in the heart of one little girl.

Speaking of legacies, several years ago I found a copy of some World War I memoirs of my grandfather, Lawrence May Sr. In them he wrote:

> We stayed in the shelter of the buildings, sniping at the enemy through the windows nearest them. They, in turn, brought up light field pieces and fired point blank through the roofs of the buildings, killing the wounded as they lay in the bakery on stretchers as well as the able-bodied soldiers who had taken refuge there.
>
> In ten minutes we had lost half of our men. We took two prisoners in the afternoon, who said that they did not see the use of fighting, since peace was about to be declared the next day. This was news to us, but we advanced no more that day.
>
> The Germans proved to be correct, orders soon came that an Armistice was to be signed at 11 o'clock the following day, instructing commanding officers to take all the ground possible before that time. Our Major, being a sensible man, balked at this, saying that he would not be the cause of one additional man losing his life, if peace was to be declared the next day. We therefore posted sentinels around the building for the night and sank into blissful sleep.

At 11 o'clock all firing ceased. We at first ventured forth cautiously then, reassured, sauntered about more freely in what had been deadly ground a few hours previously. We lined up and called the roll. As I recall it, there were but thirty-three men left in our company.

In the afternoon I led the first squad of men through the city. We had been cautioned to advance carefully, but cast all fears aside and, feeling that danger was past, marched gaily up the main street, and took up a position on the other side of the town in the rear of a chateau which had at one time been the headquarters of the Crown Prince of Germany. . . .

My first assignment at Stanay was the burial of the dead. We had taken our toll of Germans. One occurrence touched me deeply. We picked up the body of a slender, freckled-faced youth, scarcely sixteen years of age, looking as if he were hardly out of school. A few hundred yards further, we found another such lad. The resemblance to the first body we had found was so striking that I examined their identification tags. They were twin brothers, and the war had reached out and taken them only a few hours before the Armistice was declared.

As strange as this may seem, after I read Grandpa's words, I thought about Satan. I never could understand why he tries to deceive people and attempts to snatch them from God, when he knows that in the end he is the loser. Revelation 20:10 tells us, "And the devil, who deceived them, was thrown into the lake of burning sulfur, where the beast and the false prophet had been thrown. They will be tormented day and night forever and ever."

But after I read of Grandpa turning over the bodies of the twin teenage boys, I had to ask myself, "Why? Why were they killed when peace was about to be declared? Why was some mom going to be told that her two sons were killed just a few hours before the war ended?"

Grandpa explained why this had happened in his memoirs: The soldiers were to take all the ground possible.

That is exactly what Satan is doing today—taking all of the ground possible. And he wants your soul, mine, and those of our children. Our protection, as Christians, is to "put on the full armor of God so that [we] can take [our] stand against the devil's schemes" (Eph. 6:11).

We must equip our children with God's Word. It is their only hope to be ready for the fierce battles that undoubtedly lay ahead of them in the war zone called life. Be encouraged as you recall Christ's words of John 16:33: "In this world you will have trouble. But take heart! I have overcome the world."

SCRIPTURES FOR REFLECTION

Teach them to your children
and to their children after them.

DEUTERONOMY 4:9B

These commandments that I give you today are to be upon
your hearts. Impress them on your children. Talk about them
when you sit at home and when you walk along the road.

DEUTERONOMY 6:6–7

He who began a good work in you will carry it on to
completion until the day of Christ Jesus.

PHILIPPIANS 1:6

Read Proverbs 31 about the godly woman.

Questions to Ponder

1. What are the biblical values that I wish to instill in my children?

2. What am I doing on a consistent basis to instill these values in my children?

3. What steps will I take to regularly pray that the Lord will open the hearts of my children to his ways?

4. What do the following verses mean to me? Romans 10:9: "That if you confess with your mouth, 'Jesus is Lord,' and believe in your heart that God raised him from the dead, you will be saved"; and 2 Corinthians 5:17: "Therefore, if anyone is in Christ, he is a new creation; the old has gone, the new has come!"

CHAPTER 8

HELP IS ON THE WAY

. . . but there is a friend who sticks closer than a brother.

PROVERBS 18:24B

What do cars with flat tires, overgrown gardens, and my house have in common? They all need help. Working outside the home calls for more than an occasional S.O.S. Since Super Mom does not exist, we need to be willing to not only ask for help but also to accept it. And we need to reach out to others as well.

Psalm 121:1–2 gives hope as we juggle home and work responsibilities: "I lift up my eyes to the hills—where does my help come from? My help comes from the LORD, the Maker of heaven and earth." And very often he works through our husbands, friends, and neighbors to meet our needs. First Corinthians 3:9

tells us, "We are God's fellow workers; you are God's field, God's building."

I am reminded of the story of a man who had been warned that floodwaters were coming. Rather than vacating his home to higher ground, he decided to stay with it and said, "The Lord will provide for me." Sure enough, torrents of rain fell, and the water began seeping into his home. At that point, a sheriff reached the man in a rescue vehicle and warned that if he did not leave, his life would be in danger. But once again the man refused, saying, "I am going to stay with my house. The Lord will provide for me." And just as the sheriff had warned, the waters continued to rise and started to flood the entire first floor of the man's home.

Then a patrol boat roared by and words from a megaphone blared out, "Everyone must leave immediately." However, once again the man refused, saying "The Lord will provide." The waters continued to swell and the man was forced to the roof of his home. A helicopter spotted him, lowered a ladder, and someone called down, "Get on board." "No," replied the man, "the Lord will provide for me. I am going to stay with my home."

The rains continued to fall and the waters grew deeper and deeper. Finally, the man's roof was covered by several feet of water, and he drowned. When the man reached heaven, he asked God, "Lord, why didn't you answer my prayer and provide for me?" The Master replied, "Oh, I certainly did hear your prayers. I even sent a rescue vehicle, patrol boat, and a helicopter."

Moms, have you ever turned down help, thinking that you could handle things yourself? Today I would like us to consider how our husbands (for those who are married), friends, and neighbors may be the very instruments of God's help.

If you are married, your husband should not only be your best friend but also your best ally. Jim and I are really a team, and he helps me tremendously. So much so that I asked him to jot down a few ways that husbands can assist their wives who work outside the home. (Mom, you may want to leave this chapter open on the kitchen table.) However, if you are reading this book as a single working mom, take heart. God says to his own in Hebrews 13:5b, "Never will I leave you; never will I forsake you."

FROM MY HUSBAND TO YOURS

Mary asked me to share a few ways that husbands can help their working wives. I hope at least a few of these suggestions will help you.

- Be your wife's best friend—someone she can share joy and frustration with. Other than with Jesus Christ, there should be no closer relationship (Eph. 5:31).
- Make sure your wife is held in high esteem and respect in the eyes of your children (Prov. 22:6).
- Accept spiritual leadership. Seek what God would want you to do and apply everything to that grid.
- Have your own quiet time. Admit your dependency upon God and renew yourself through the Scriptures. Before you can be helpful, you need to confess that you are helpless.
- Pray daily with your wife.
- Have reasonable expectations. Don't expect everything to always be neat and dust-free at home. Remember, dust does not spoil! I once heard someone say that it does reach a state of equilibrium. After enough gathers, when people leave the house, they tend to carry off as much as they brought in!

- Be affirming. Notice the things she does that are "ordinary" and tell her how much you appreciate them. It's easy to see things that aren't exactly up to par. Avoid verbalizing what your wife already knows. This may take some effort, but it is worth it.
- Lend a helping hand—especially in ways that you don't ordinarily think of as "your area," such as vacuuming, washing clothes, cleaning bathrooms, or grocery shopping. (You may end up grocery shopping only once.) Philippians 2:3–4 reminds us, "Do nothing out of selfish ambition or vain conceit, but in humility consider others better than yourselves. Each of you should look not only to your own interests, but also to the interests of others."
- Volunteer for chores instead of being asked. She'll appreciate it more if you do.
- Stay away from comments like "Gee, you look tired." While honesty is the best policy, a working mom does not want to hear such remarks.
- Take her out—to eat, to the movies. A weekly date night is a good idea, and it will help the two of you communicate better. It may be the best opportunity you have all week to really pay attention to your wife.
- Buy her an occasional surprise "thank-you" gift. It does not need to be extravagant—a card or flowers are nice. It is really the thought that counts.
- Cook a special meal from time to time. I like to grill—and even get a little creative in the kitchen. Acknowledge that this is for her, not because the meals have been lacking.

- Let her sleep in occasionally, even if she says she isn't tired. Many of us don't know how fatigued we really are, especially if we're running a busy schedule. If she sleeps in, do some chores so she won't feel like she has less of a day to do things.
- Fix breakfast on some Saturday mornings. Getting up before sunrise for something other than hunting or fishing never hurt anybody.
- A marriage relationship will include some disagreements, just be sure to keep short accounts. Colossians 3:12–14 tells us, "Therefore, as God's chosen people, holy and dearly loved, clothe yourselves with compassion, kindness, humility, gentleness and patience. Bear with each other and forgive whatever grievances you may have against one another. Forgive as the Lord forgave you. And over all these virtues put on love, which binds them all together in perfect unity."
- Have some fun. I have already mentioned a date night, but don't forget to laugh daily.
- Learn not to unload your own frustrations on your spouse as soon as you see her. Give her time to unwind before bringing up anything negative.
- Work out your schedule so you can go to your children's activities—especially if Mom can't. That may involve some financial sacrifice, particularly if you are self-employed like I am. But what you gain in memories is well worth the cost.
- Be a good financial partner. If you don't know how to set up a budget, get help. Ask your ac-

countant or insurance agent for advice concerning what things to consider in long-range planning. Most of all, be a responsible spender. Debt is generally not good.

- Get your children involved in helping around the house. When they're little, they love to help. When they are older, they may need to get reacquainted with family chores. Teaching your children to help others is biblical and priceless.
- Plan some special activities for your children. Spending time with Dad is good, and it gives Mom a break and some needed space. This applies not only to younger children, but also to teenagers.
- Learn to say no. There are a lot of things that pull on our time, and many are worthwhile. But overloading on activities can lead to scheduling difficulties, financial expense, fatigue, and short tempers.

FROM ONE SINGLE MOM TO ANOTHER

As promised, here are some hints to single moms from other single moms whose hearts are at home:

- You cannot build a loving home for your children until you can put aside any resentment that you feel toward your ex-spouse. This is important because their father will always be their father. You will have to deal with him, and possibly with his new spouse. How you handle this will be the difference between a peaceful home and a home in a war zone. ("Then Peter came to Jesus and asked, 'Lord, how many times shall

I forgive my brother when he sins against me? Up to seven times?' Jesus answered, 'I tell you, not seven times, but seventy-seven times'" [Matt. 18:21–22].)

- The one thing that I have learned as a single mom is that, after God, my children have to come first. They need to know that I love them at all times, and they need to feel safe.

- We try and keep the house picked up during the week so we can play all weekend. (And yes, sometimes clothes will be left on the bedroom floor and there may be a few dishes in the kitchen sink.)

- Every morning I say 'I love you' to my daughter. I fix breakfast, take her to the bus stop, and make sure I know where she will be in the afternoon. I let her interrupt me at work every afternoon to talk with me about school. When I am leaving work, I call to let her know that I am on my way home.

- Since my teenage son lives with his dad, I phone him at least twice a week to let him know that I am thinking of him and to listen to him.

- It is very hard when one parent does not have the same spiritual values as the other. It's difficult when the kids go to church when they are with me, but do not attend church when they are with their father. When one of the children asks me, "Dad makes me say I am only 12 (when she is 14); why don't you?" I just say, what did God tell you to do? Did He not say, "Thou shalt not lie"? Then I ask them what is the right thing to do.

- I learned the hard way that if your ex-husband makes five times as much money as you do, don't try to outspend on Christmas or birthdays.
- I have to remind myself that my ex-husband is not a believer. Although I cannot change him, God sure can. I think it is important to pray for my ex-husband, and to model this in front of my kids.

God often uses our loved ones and friends to lift us up in day-to-day life. But have you ever thought that he also provides great encouragement through the examples of godly women in Scripture?

FROM WOMEN WHO HAVE GONE BEFORE US

Let's take a few moments now and examine the faithfulness of three mothers: Jochebed (Moses' mother, Exodus 6:20), Hannah (Samuel's mother, 1 Samuel 1:20), and Mary (the mother of Jesus, Matthew 1:16).

Jochebed, the mother of Moses

Now a man of the house of Levi married a Levite woman, and she became pregnant and gave birth to a son. When she saw that he was a fine child, she hid him for three months. But when she could hide him no longer, she got a papyrus basket for him and coated it with tar and pitch. Then she placed the child in it and put it among the reeds along the bank of the Nile (Exod. 2:1–3).

You will recall Pharaoh's order that every newborn Hebrew son be cast into the river. Moses' mother (Jochebed) recognized that little Moses was not an ordinary child (Heb. 11:23). So by faith, she placed him lovingly into a tar-covered basket—trusting that somehow his life would be spared as she sent him on his early journey down the Nile.

Although Jochebed knew that she could not protect her young son from death, she could entrust him to the hands of God. Moses' future was out of her control, but it was very much in the control of a sovereign God.

Hannah, the mother of Samuel

"O LORD Almighty, if you will only look upon your servant's misery and remember me, and not forget your servant but give her a son, then I will give him to the LORD for all the days of his life" (1 Sam. 1:11).

Hannah, the wife of Elkanah, had been barren. She vowed that if God would only give her a son, then she would give him back to the Lord. God heard her prayer and blessed her with a son named Samuel. After Hannah had weaned little Samuel, she was true to her promise and entrusted him to Eli, the high priest.

Imagine praying for years that the Lord would open your barren womb—and then finally to be blessed with a child. How difficult it must have been for Hannah to have given her little boy to Eli. After all, Eli's own sons, Hophni and Phinehas, were not godly men. But Hannah did not put her trust in Eli to raise little Samuel. Hannah trusted God to work through even a man such as Eli.

Mary, the mother of Jesus

In the sixth month, God sent the angel Gabriel to Nazareth, a town in Galilee, to a virgin pledged to be married to a man named Joseph, a descendant of David. The virgin's name was Mary. . . . But the angel said to her, "Do not be afraid, Mary, you have found favor with God. You will be with child and give birth to a son, and you are to give him the name Jesus" (Luke 1:26–27, 30–31).

And if I had been Mary—a teenager engaged to be married—how would I have reacted when an angel told me that I would give birth to the very Son of God? After all, my life was planned. I was going to marry a wonderful man named Joseph. How could I be pregnant? I was a virgin. And how could Joseph understand? What would people say?

But instead of doubt and worry, Mary believed the angel. She chose to have absolute faith in God rather than to fear man.

* * *

Mom, when you are trying your best to raise your kids alone; when you are dog-tired after a long day at work and the baby wakes up at 2 A.M. and then again at 4 A.M.; when your teenager does not know whether to go to college or to get a job—what's a mom to do?

Well, if we look to Jochebed, Hannah, and Mary, we'll recognize that the only sure thing we can do is trust and obey God. These women focused on the Lord rather than on their circumstances.

We should make it a habit to turn to Scripture when we need direction. The words of Psalm 56:3 tell us, "When I am afraid, I will trust in you. In God, whose word I praise, in God I trust; I will not be afraid. What can mortal man do to me?"

Yes, help does come from our husbands and from one another. But more importantly, it comes from the Lord. And because we are his children, He will never leave us. He will never fail us.

SCRIPTURES FOR REFLECTION

Freely you have received, freely give.

MATTHEW 10:8B

*Do nothing out of selfish ambition or vain conceit, but
in humility consider others better than yourselves.*

PHILIPPIANS 2:3

Read the prayer for strength in Ephesians 3.

QUESTIONS TO PONDER

1. If you are married answer the following questions,
   and then discuss them with your husband:
   - What are three specific ways that my husband
     has helped me during the past week?

   - What are two specific ways that my husband
     could help me?

   - What areas of my life seem to weigh me down?

   - How could my load be lightened?

2. If you are a single mom, please answer these questions:
   - Where have I accepted help in the last week?

- What areas of my life encourage me?

- What areas of my life weigh me down?

- Who can I ask to help me lighten my load?

3. What has the Lord said to me through our study of Jochebed, Hannah, and Mary?

4. How can I apply this lesson to my daily life?

5. What does my life say about my willingness to both give and receive? What changes do I need to make in either of these two areas?

CHAPTER 9

HOW CAN WORKING MOMS NETWORK?

The only way to have a friend is to be one.

RALPH WALDO EMERSON

I have good news! You and I do not have to try to be Super Moms because we are part of the body of Christ. To better understand what this means, let's look at 1 Corinthians 12:12–22:

> The body is a unit, though it is made up of many parts; and though all its parts are many, they form one body. So it is with Christ. For we were all baptized by one Spirit into one body—whether Jew or Greek, slave or free—and we were all given the one Spirit to drink.
>
> Now the body is not made up of one part but of many. If the foot should say, "Because I am not a hand, I do not belong to the body," it would not for

that reason cease to be part of the body. And if the ear should say, "Because I am not an eye, I do not belong to the body," it would not for that reason cease to be part of the body. If the whole body were an eye, where would the sense of hearing be? If the whole body were an ear, where would the sense of smell be? But in fact God has arranged the parts in the body, every one of them, just as he wanted them to be. If they were all one part, where would the body be? As it is, there are many parts, but one body.

The eye cannot say to the hand, "I don't need you!" And the head cannot say to the feet, "I don't need you!" On the contrary, those parts of the body that seem to be weaker are indispensable.

Mom, we need each other. And God has uniquely gifted each of us as Christians: "For we are God's workmanship, created in Christ Jesus to do good works, which God prepared in advance for us to do" (Eph. 2:10).

Many times I have begun a day thinking, *OK, Mary, God has already prepared some good works for you today. Now, just recognize where he wants to work through you.* When I do this, it is really exciting to recognize his divine hand.

I vividly remember one day when I was at work and a harried stay-at-home mother exited the elevator. I knew the expression on her face—she was battle-weary from motherhood. Her husband was traveling, and she had no relatives in town.

It was almost as if God tapped me on the shoulder and said, "Mary, she needs some help. Offer to watch her kids."

"Oh, Lord," was my initial response, "you know I don't have time to do that right now. I've got my own family, and with work and everything, there are just not enough hours in the day."

Then it seemed that the Holy Spirit personally reminded me of the Good Samaritan (Luke 10:25–37). You probably recall the story: A priest and Levite passed by a man who had been beaten by robbers. They did not stop. But a Samaritan did take the time to bandage the injured man's wounds, place him on his own donkey, and take him to an inn. The Samaritan went the extra mile to help someone in need.

I got the message and did not want to be like the priest and Levite.

OK, Lord, I inwardly said, *I will let your Spirit work through me, and I will offer to help.*

Well, this mom accepted my offer with great appreciation. And on Saturday afternoon she very willingly left her home in my hands. All I did was play with her kids; we had a blast. And it was amazing—somehow I completed all of my own household chores before noon—unheard of!

What a blessing I received by simply being available for God's purposes. I received much more than I gave.

WHAT EXACTLY IS NETWORKING?

When we network with others, we recognize that we need each other. Let me give some tangible examples of how we moms can work together for the benefit of our families.

I remember one terrible, horrible, no-good morning when I could not find my car keys. Jim was out of town. The boys were already at school. What could I do? Well, I called a dear neighbor who was more than happy to take me to work. When our children were younger, this same neighbor and I would freely call each other when we needed someone to watch our kids while we went to the doctor or ran errands.

We have some other wonderful friends, Doyle and Colleen Stewart, who mean a lot to our family. Mr. Stewart is now in his nineties. It seems like yesterday when he would talk with our boys over the fence and give them gum. Our little guys would run and greet him by saying, "Mr. Stewart! Mr. Stewart!"

Over the years, it has become increasingly difficult for Mr. Stewart to mow his lawn. And so, reluctantly, he has allowed Chris and John to mow it for him. Through this, our family has learned not only how to give, but also how to receive.

You see, Mr. Stewart often knocks on our door, giving the boys a John Wayne movie, some cold drinks, or fruit. He has allowed Chris and John to know what it is like to willingly look after a neighbor—expecting nothing in return. No price tag could be put on this. Our family has also experienced the joy of receiving when we accept Mr. Stewart's gifts of appreciation to our family. As we give and receive, we are channels of Christ's love—parts of the body of Christ in action.

There have been times when colleagues have needed help getting vehicles to and from repair shops. And times when Jim and I have needed someone to help us get a vehicle to and from repair shops, and to and from repair shops, and to and from repair shops. (You know you are in trouble when everyone at the repair shop knows you on a first-name basis.)

Whenever the kids have signed up for sports, I have always tried to get to know the other parents and learn who lives near us for car pool purposes. We have brought other kids to and from practices and games, and other parents have done the same for us. We do not keep score of who does what.

One year, when our boys were in junior high, we carpooled with some families who lived nearby. We brought the children to school in the mornings, and another mom brought them home in the afternoons. That year, there was one mom who could not participate in the car pool. Despite this, she often needed someone to drop her junior-high son home after school. Since her home was on our route, we just brought him to his home—expecting no reciprocation.

There were times when Jim and I went out of town for a weekend and needed someone to watch our boys. We initiated calls to friends who were happy to have two young houseguests for the weekend. And there have been times when others have asked us to do the same for them. In today's busy world, we need each other more than ever.

HOW TO NETWORK

If you are wondering, "Who can I network with?" then you probably need to make some more friends. Get involved in a Bible study. (I do this during my lunch hour.) Volunteer at your child's school—help with class parties and work in concession stands. Get to know your neighbors. Offer to be a "team mom" and help with phone calls. We have to be friends to have friends.

Our office has what we call "Women's Fellowship." The ladies meet monthly at noon to socialize, and generally we have a speaker. Meetings have highlighted such topics as flower arranging, decorating your home, balancing checkbooks, business etiquette, and growing spiritually in the midst of challenges. Some months we just go to lunch together at a nearby restaurant. But through this informal organization, we have formed friendships and developed teamwork. Perhaps you will want to organize such a group for your place of employment.

Networking can be as simple as picking up the phone and asking for advice. I have asked others about parenting, school activities, choosing a summer camp for our children, and even how to prepare our children for college. Even the writing of this book would have been impossible without the help of many of my friends.

On the first day of John's senior year, the parents of one of his friends invited a small group of seniors and their moms and dads to their home. The kids shared their expectations for their senior year and future plans. And the parents shared the pride and joy that they had for their children. What a great way for one generation to affirm another.

Another couple took several kids (including John) skiing over spring break. Parents and kids met together to discuss expectations and needs. Take the time to get to know not only your kids' friends, but also their parents. It's invaluable. To me, friendship is the foundation for involvement with others—the basis for networking.

I have participated in groups of moms preparing other moms for their kids' release to college. Wonderful hints were shared and friendships were formed. Ideas were given for decorating dorm rooms, collegiate "needs vs. wants," communication, financial considerations, etc. How great it is to learn from those who have gone before us, and to teach those who will follow us.

At our boys' elementary and junior high schools, moms' groups were organized for prayer. When our boys entered high school, no such group existed for their particular school, so another mom and I organized what we called "Golden Links." After meeting with the school's administrator and receiving his approval, we sent an introductory flyer to parents in the school's newsletter.

We explained that "Golden Links" was an outreach by moms and dads to encourage the school staff and faculty through prayers, notes of encouragement, and occasional treats. Parents could indicate their desires to pray for and encourage a particular teacher or staff member.

This outreach has grown over the years and now meets quarterly to pray corporately for the school. It also sponsors an annual "teacher appreciation luncheon." How uplifting it has been for the school's faculty and staff to know that parents are standing behind them, regularly praying for their needs and encouraging them with occasional notes and treats. And through this informal group, hearts have been knit together. People know that others are truly just a phone call away.

James 5:16 tells us that "the prayer of a righteous man is powerful and effective." When you are facing a particularly tough day at home or at the office, share your concerns and ask someone to pray for you. I have done this countless times, and it is so comforting to know that someone is praying for me during the very time when I have a particularly difficult task to face.

Jim and I have been part of small groups that have studied Scripture and prayed together about the needs of our families. We have attended numerous conferences sponsored by our church that have helped us build a strong marriage, learn how to be better parents, and anticipate the teen years. All of these things help us connect with others.

Networking. People helping people. The body of Christ in action.

NETWORKING IN SCRIPTURE

When I think of networking and helping one another, I am reminded of Dorcas. We are told in Acts 9 how she took care of widows and made clothing for them. Dorcas reached out to women in need.

When Pharaoh's daughter rescued baby Moses from the Nile, Moses' sister asked her, "Shall I go and get one of the Hebrew women to nurse the baby for you?" (Exod. 2:7). She said yes, and Moses' mother was brought to nurse her own son. Pharaoh's daughter needed help, and God provided Moses' own mother to help her.

Titus 2 tells us that older women are to teach younger women: "They can train the younger women to love their husbands and children, to be self-controlled and pure, to be busy at home, to be kind, and to be subject to their husbands, so that no one will malign the word of God" (Titus 2:4–5). This picture of mentoring shows how God uses people to pass down his truths about what's truly important about families and life.

I have always loved the story of the Israelites fighting the Amalekites. We are told in Exodus 17:10–13: "So Joshua fought the Amalekites as Moses had ordered, and Moses, Aaron and Hur went to the top of the hill. As long as Moses held up his hands, the Israelites were winning, but whenever he lowered his hands, the Amalekites were winning. When Moses' hands grew tired, they took a stone and put it under him and he sat on it. Aaron and Hur held his hands up—one on one side, one on the other—so that his hands remained steady till sunset. So Joshua overcame the Amalekite army with the sword."

Mom, just as Moses had to have someone hold his hands so that Joshua could defeat the Amalekites, so too do we need others to come alongside us and hold our hands. We must practice giving and receiving, for God wants us to do both. As we allow Christ to do his good works through us and others, we will truly be a picture of the body of Christ at work for the glory of God.

Have you ever considered what would have happened if no one had been willing to hold up Moses' hands? What would have happened if Moses refused their help, choosing instead to "just do it himself"? I believe, in either of these situations, that the Israelites would have been defeated by the Amalekites. God wants us not only to help one another, but also to admit when we ourselves need some help.

GOD IS AT WORK THROUGH US

Psalm 121:1–2 tells us, "I lift up my eyes to the hills—where does my help come from? My help comes from the LORD, the Maker of heaven and earth." When we recognize this truth, then we are ready to lift others' burdens and let them lift ours.

For the Lord himself is orchestrating situations, using men and women as his channels of love and comfort. As we are told in 1 Peter 4:10: "Each one should use whatever gift he has received to serve others, faithfully administering God's grace in its various forms."

Mom, as we reach out to others and also allow others to help us, we are developing rich friendships. And God very well could be orchestrating special relationships in your life and mine for the express purpose of bringing others to faith in Jesus Christ. Rather than living inward lives we must reach out to a hurting world. By our willingness to not only give, but also to receive, we can hold up others' hands on those particularly battle-weary days. And they can hold up ours. We need each other!

Let's take a quick review of some networking ideas that might even help you today:

- Get involved in a Bible study.
- Get to know the parents of kids who participate with your child in sporting events. Learn who lives near you for car pool purposes.
- Volunteer at your child's school. Help with class parties and work in concession stands.
- Meet with parents of your children's friends to discuss plans and expectations.
- Brainstorm with moms who have released their children to junior high school, high school, and college. This will help you anticipate these phases in the life of your child.
- Pray with other moms for your children's schools.
- Regularly meet with a group of women from your office to share tips about balancing home and work responsibilities.

SCRIPTURES FOR REFLECTION

A man reaps what he sows.

GALATIANS 6:7B

Love your neighbor as yourself.

LEVITICUS 19:18

Do nothing out of selfish ambition or vain conceit,
but in humility consider others better than yourselves.
Each of you should look not only to your own interests,
but also to the interests of others.

PHILIPPIANS 2:3–4

Read 1 Corinthians 12:12–31 about the body of Christ.

QUESTIONS TO PONDER

1. What are several ways that I can help others? (If possible, write down the names of specific people and how you can help them.)

2. In what areas do I need help? (If possible, write the names of people who could help you.)

3. What does God's Word say about how we should love our neighbors? (Consider Romans 12:10–13, "Be devoted to one another in brotherly love. Honor one another above yourselves. Never be lacking in zeal, but keep your spiritual fervor, serving the Lord. Be joyful in hope, patient in affliction, faithful in prayer. Share with God's people who are in need. Practice hospitality.")

4. What is one thing I can do for another mother this week that would lighten her load?

5. How do I allow others to experience the joy of giving by my receiving?

6. How am I willing to ask others to "hold up my hands" when I am in the midst of daily battles?

CHAPTER 10

LESSONS FROM THE HEART

As for man, his days are like grass,
he flourishes like a flower of the field;
the wind blows over it and it is gone,
and its place remembers it no more.

Through the years, my thoughts have matured concerning time, true wealth, and humor. I would like to share some lessons I have learned over the decades—from my heart to yours.

DAYS ARE LIKE GRASS

As for man, his days are like grass,
he flourishes like a flower of the field;
the wind blows over it and it is gone,
and its place remembers it no more.

PSALM 103:15–16

When you were a child waiting for the arrival of a birthday or Christmas, didn't time seem to creep by? Someone recently told me that her young son moaned, "Mom, it's four weeks until Christmas." Her response was, "I cannot believe it is just four weeks until Christmas!" Yes, as the years pass, our impression of time begins to change.

When I was a new college graduate, I recall knowing couples who had been married for five years—this seemed like a very long time to me. But after all, I had been in college for four years, so maybe it is understandable why five years would have seemed like such an enormous period of time.

I recall when we were told that our first baby, Chris, could come home from the hospital. (You'll remember that he was born prematurely and had to stay in the neonatal unit for a month after his birth.) Looking at this little life, and realizing that God had given him to Jim and me to raise—well, it was such a feeling of responsibility. And to think that he would be in our home for at least eighteen years. This seemed like a lifetime! But after all, I was in my twenties; it's no wonder that eighteen years seemed like a lifetime.

Then shortly after Chris was born, my grandfather died. Although he was in his eighties, I felt that he had lived forever. Yet when my own dad went to be with the Lord almost twenty years later, it seemed as though I was just beginning to get to really know him. And Dad was seventy-six years old.

The passage of days into weeks, and weeks into years, and years into decades has a way of changing our perspective. We are told in Psalm 90:12, "Teach us to number our days aright, that we may gain a heart of wisdom." Second Peter 3:8 tells us, "But do not forget this one thing, dear friends: With the Lord a day is like a thousand years, and a thousand years are like a day." Only when I focus on eternity and God's plan for his own, can I begin to grasp how I can number my days.

Today, birthday and Christmas celebrations seem to roll into one another. Jim and I have been married for almost a quarter of a century. Our son Chris is now in his twenties, and John is entering college. What I had thought would be an eternity of child-rearing years has vanished overnight. It's true; time does go by quickly. May we help our children appreciate life, and treasure even the simplest things.

When our boys were younger, we tried to use nature to help us appreciate the wonder of God's creation. We generally found a cocoon or two during the spring. After putting them in a jar (with holes), we'd watch until we saw signs of life emerging. Then we would remove the cocoons from the jar and watch the miracle of life in action.

We could not help the emerging butterfly get out more easily from the cocoon. If we did, the butterfly's wings would be too weak and he would die. As he literally fought his way and pumped his wings, he gained strength. What an amazing reminder that there will be individual battles in life. But we can grow from them if we will just keep our focus on God's purpose for us.

Proverbs 29:18 tells us, "Where there is no vision, the people perish" (KJV). Likewise, when there is vision, the people live. When we focus on eternity (an eternity perspective), then we have a grasp of Christ's high purpose for us in our homes. No matter our occupations—attorney, bank teller, secretary, writer, physician—none surpasses the charge God has given us as moms. He has entrusted us to nurture and train the next generation. We must place our relationships with our Lord and our families before those in either the community or at work. Relationships take effort—whether they be with our Maker, family, or friends. And I think you will agree that working outside the home does take extra energy and requires a great deal of planning.

We truly need to begin each day in God's Word, asking him to show us how we can spend our time wisely. We cannot go back and regain tomorrow; but we do have today. May you and I heed the words of Psalm 89:47: "Remember how fleeting is my life." May we face life with an eternity perspective, realizing that we are truly pilgrims in a foreign land, and that our true home is heaven. Since our lives are like grass, here today and gone tomorrow, may we make our days really count.

The Lilies Do Not Toil or Spin

Consider how the lilies grow. They do not labor or spin. Yet I
tell you, not even Solomon in all his splendor was dressed
like one of these. If that is how God clothes the grass of the
field, which is here today, and tomorrow is thrown into the
fire, how much more will he clothe you, O you of little faith!

LUKE 12:27–28

Last summer our son John and I went on a mission trip to Mexico. It was sobering to see firsthand the crude shacks that some people call home. I am sure almost any home in the U.S. would have seemed like a mansion to those living in such meager dwellings. Being in such a poverty-stricken area made me think, *Are things our most valuable possessions?* Picture men and women who have lost their hearing or sight. What material possessions would they trade to once again hear or see? Probably all they had. And if your child were diagnosed with cancer, would you spare any expense to find the best physicians and most advanced care?

I've heard people question why God allows poverty. As I have gotten older, I have realized that the worst type of poverty is not a lack of material things. Rather it is a heart that refuses to accept God and is cold to spiritual matters. Relationships and our abilities to see and hear and touch are far more valuable than mere possessions.

Before you make any decisions concerning where you should live, what you should wear, and what you should eat, ask yourself, "What is truly valuable in my life?" May God give us eternity perspectives that help us choose what is truly valuable in his kingdom.

A TIME TO LAUGH

There is a time for everything,
and a season for every activity under heaven: . . .
a time to laugh.

ECCLESIASTES 3:1, 4A

Doesn't it feel good to laugh? Someone once said that "laughter does the heart good." And yet sometimes, with family and work demands and the hectic pace of life, I need to be reminded of this. When I recall humorous times, it makes me relax and smile.

We have funny family stories that resurface year after year. When John was just a toddler, he climbed out of his crib and down the stairs. He reached his destination—the kitchen. He had a smile of glee on his face when he was finally discovered. It seemed like every box of cereal and box of instant potatoes had been emptied onto the floor. That day we chose to laugh at a little boy's great adventure, and clean up the mess later.

I remember one child saying that he did not want to be in a "car pool." I couldn't understand why until he said, "Mrs. Jones has a car pool and I don't want a car pool." You see, the Joneses had a station wagon, and he did not like station wagons. Obviously, we were not communicating.

Then there was the day when several children were arguing over how many donut holes they wanted. Finally one child piped in saying, "I don't care how many donut holes you get, because there's nothing in a donut hole!"

It is so good to just relax and smile at life around us. Once a little girl who was staying at our house remarked after she had taken a bite of cotton candy, "It's cotton and somehow it turns into candy in your mouth." When Chris had his first fortune cookie he said, "I liked the cookie, but the paper was really hard to chew." And there was the time when my sister asked her daughter why she wanted to be on the soccer team (since she did not like to run or get hot), and she said, "Because I like orange slices and the uniforms are cute." (No, she did not play soccer that year.) And we've all probably enjoyed watching little baseball players drawing in the dirt when they were supposed to be watching for balls.

Our family also enjoys telling stories on our animals. We have dog stories galore—the dog who burped at the mailman and also got stuck under the coffee table; the dog who got a bone stuck on his lower lip; and the one who was panic stricken when he accidentally fell over a decorative fence and found himself out of our yard.

Life can be so serious at times, and it is just good for us to laugh. We need to look for the humor around us. Humor can be the silver lining that gets us through the day with a smile on our faces.

Over the years, I have kept a "funny file" at work. Again, when things just seem a bit heavy, it is wonderful to pull it out and just smile a little. Allow me to share a couple of "treasures" with you:

E-mail message: "Please note that if you place a candy cane in an envelope that has a stamp on it, the candy cane will be smashed as it goes through the canceling machine at the post office. This makes for a very messy Christmas card."

During a severe snowstorm, one Red Cross rescue team was carried by helicopter to within a mile of a cabin that was all but covered by a deep snowdrift.

The rescuers struggled on foot through the deep snowdrifts and finally arrived at the cabin, where they shoveled away enough snow to clear the door. They knocked, and when their summons was answered by a mountaineer, one rescuer stepped up and said, "We're from the Red Cross."

"Well," said the man, scratching his head, "it's been a right tough winter and I don't think we can give anything this year."

Of course, we moms love to share funny things that the kids say. One day a colleague of mine was wearing a very stylish suit that had what is called "poodle cloth" for a collar. She said her young son had asked her what the collar was made with. When she responded, "Poodle cloth," he said, "You mean, they killed a poodle for that?"

This same little boy also asked his mom, "Did they have dogs when you were a little girl?"

And then there was the day when Jim heard a popping sound, followed by a horrible smell permeating the house. Jim even wondered if a sewage pipe had burst. Finally, he located the source of our problem: John had gone fishing and had left chicken livers in his tackle box for about two weeks. Do you know what happens to chicken livers after they have been in a tackle box for two weeks? Well, we sure do!

As my friend Gloria Cates said, "Normal is only a setting on a dryer." We must not take ourselves too seriously and should be willing to smile at the curve balls that are thrown our way.

Have you ever enjoyed watching your kids at play or work, unbeknownst to them? I remember watching John one day when he was about six. He had seen a poster of a dog hooked up to a wagon, and Jim guessed that he was going to mimic this. Sure enough, John became the "cowboy" and Sunny, "the great stallion pulling a wagon." It was a funny sight to behold.

Proverbs 17:22 reminds us that "A cheerful heart is good medicine, but a crushed spirit dries up the bones." May God help us have cheerful hearts and homes that radiate warmth, comfort, and love.

So, from my heart to yours: May you have an eternity focus, valuing what God values, and keeping a smile on your face.

SCRIPTURES FOR REFLECTION

Are not two sparrows sold for a penny? Yet not one of them
will fall to the ground apart from the will of your Father.
And even the very hairs of your head are all numbered. So
don't be afraid; you are worth more than many sparrows.
MATTHEW 10:29–31

Teach us to number our days aright,
that we may gain a heart of wisdom.
PSALM 90:12

But man, despite his riches, does not endure;
he is like the beasts that perish.
PSALM 49:12

Oh, the depth of the riches of the wisdom
and knowledge of God!
ROMANS 11:33A

Our mouths were filled with laughter,
our tongues with songs of joy.
PSALM 126:2

QUESTIONS TO PONDER

1. What does God value?

2. What do I value in life?

3. Where am I investing my time?

4. At this time of my life, how am I trying to seek God's will for my family?

5. How have I demonstrated to my children this week/month how I wisely spend the resources God has entrusted to me?

6. In what situations this week have I taken time to laugh and enjoy life?

CHAPTER 11

WHAT CHILD IS THIS?

Depend upon it—God's work done
in God's way will never lack supplies.

J. HUDSON TAYLOR

You are probably familiar with the Christmas song that begins "What Child is this. . . ." Of course, the writer was referring to the Christ child and the incomprehensible truth that he was fully God and fully man and came to earth to be our Redeemer.

Have you ever looked at your child and wondered, "What child is this?" If you have more than one child, or even if you have been with more than one child for several hours, you can affirm that children differ greatly in their responses to life. Redheads or brunettes, dark complexion or fair, 18 inches or 4 feet, shy or aggressive—kids come in a variety of sizes, shapes, and dispositions. What's a mom to do?

Proverbs 22:6 tells us to "train a child in the way he should go, and when he is old he will not turn from it." This verse does not guarantee that our children will accept Christ as their Savior just because we are Christians and take them to church. It does mean that if we recognize how God has uniquely made our children, and train them according to their uniqueness, then the training will shape and mold the people they become.

IDENTIFY YOUR CHILD'S "BENT"

Dr. Duane Cuthbertson wrote,

> We have already seen that Proverbs 22:6 may be paraphrased, "Modify the will of the child, the way he is bent, and when he gets to be a teenager, that pattern will stay with him."
> Note that we must modify the will according to the way the child is "bent." Modifying the will of a compliant child will be much different from attempting the same with a defiant one. We need to understand the "bent"—the predisposition—of each of our children, as well as the source of that bent. *(Raising Your Child, Not Your Voice* [Wheaton, Ill.: Victor Books, 1987], 72)

Sounds easy enough, doesn't it? But when you are dealing with a one-of-a-kind son or daughter, parenting is anything but easy. But be encouraged, Psalm 139:13–16 tells us:

> *For you created my inmost being;*
> *you knit me together in my mother's womb.*
> *I praise you because I am fearfully and wonderfully made;*
> *your works are wonderful, I know that full well.*
> *My frame was not hidden from you*
> *when I was made in the secret place.*
> *When I was woven together in the depths of the earth,*

your eyes saw my unformed body.
All the days ordained for me
were written in your book before one of them came to be.

Many years ago a professional musician played the harp at our church. She was wearing a beautiful handmade sweater and said that it reminded her of Psalm 139—every fiber of that sweater had been personally touched by her mother. Mom, every fiber of your being and mine, of our husband and children, has been woven together by our Creator, the Lord Almighty. What comfort that gives me.

Why then can parenting be such a challenge? All we have to do is understand the bent of our children and raise them appropriately, and presto—we will raise a godly man or woman whose life and actions point others to Christ. But it's not that easy, is it?

God is the one who wove our children together. And his thoughts and ways are not ours (Isa. 55:8). How then can we grasp the bent of our children and raise them as God desires? The answer lies in time—time spent seeking God's wisdom through the Scriptures and prayer, and spending time with our children.

And doesn't it seem that some children require less effort to raise than others? Personally, I think those who are more like us are easier to train because we can understand them. But don't despair when it comes to raising a child who appears difficult to you, for it is this very child who will bring you to your knees. You will know that you do not have the answers. And you will grow closer to the Lord and strengthen your own walk with him in the process.

We have raised two sons and have also parented several foster children. They have all been different. For example, as the kids entered the teenage years, they were given more freedoms. However, they had to let us know where they were and who they were with. I remember how easy this was for one child. If he would leave a friend's home and go to a restaurant, he would just pick up the phone and let us know his plans. But for another child, this seemed like an invasion of his privacy.

The worst punishment for one child was taking away phone privileges, while another could not have cared less about the phone. Some children felt that being sent to their room for thirty minutes was unusually cruel punishment, while others would have loved this as discipline. Some children would come to Jim and me for advice before they undertook big tasks, others just "did it themselves." When given the choice of going to the zoo or playing in the backyard, one child chose the backyard. Some kids loved to swim; others would rather be catching fly balls. One of our boys really enjoyed playing with his toys, another reveled in taking them apart. Every child is different.

I find great comfort in Romans 8:28: "And we know that in all things God works for the good of those who love him, who have been called according to his purpose." Although Jim and I have tried to raise our children in a godly manner, we have made plenty of mistakes. But I recognize that God is sovereign, and I know that Jim, our sons, and I are Christians. We each have grown in our love for Christ and in the knowledge of his will, and I am confident that God will weave our successes and failures into something very good that will bring him glory and praise.

LEARN THE LANGUAGE

There are many great resources available to Christian parents today. Gary Chapman and Ross Campbell have written a wonderful book entitled *The Five Love Languages of Children*, which I highly recommend. They said, "You can simply remember that behavioral expressions of love can be divided into physical touch, quality time, gifts, acts of service, and words of affirmation" ([Chicago: Moody Press, 1997], 27).

Jim and I discussed these five expressions of love with Chris and John, and we talked about which was their "language." Initially, John said acts of service. But several months after reading Chapman and Ross's book, I heard Sandy Smith (from Fielder Road Baptist Church in Arlington, Texas) speak about love languages. She said to consider how people express love themselves to help determine their language of expressing love. It was as though the lights finally came on for me, and I realized that our son John feels affirmed by gifts, not by acts of service.

Now, honestly, I would have said that anyone who speaks in "gifts" must be a very materialistic person. After all, where does anyone give gifts in the Bible?

Ah, turn to John 12:1–3: "Six days before the Passover, Jesus arrived at Bethany, where Lazarus lived, whom Jesus had raised from the dead. Here a dinner was given in Jesus' honor. Martha served, while Lazarus was among those reclining at the table with him. Then Mary took about a pint of pure nard, an expensive perfume; she poured it on Jesus' feet and wiped his feet with her hair. And the house was filled with the fragrance of the perfume."

And we are told of the most valuable gift ever in Romans 6:23: "For the wages of sin is death, but the gift of God is eternal life in Christ Jesus our Lord."

As I thought about John, I realized that he loves to give gifts in creative ways—sending people on elaborate scavenger hunts or enclosing a simple present within multiple boxes. I recall how he gave his brother a huge, heavy box one Christmas. We were traveling that year for the holidays, and I remember Jim somehow finding room in the trunk of the car for this Christmas treasure. Well, I cannot tell you what John actually gave Chris that year, but I do remember what seems like boxes within boxes within boxes, assorted papers and ribbons, and fi-nally—the last "package" with Chris's gift (perhaps a signed baseball card) wrapped with a brick!

Jim and I give all the usual gifts. As the boys have become teenagers, we have often just given them money as gifts, so they can buy whatever they want. But when I recognized that John's main love language is gifts, I realized that we have slighted him. How could we remedy this? Well, on our dog's birthday (Hey, he was born at our house. Who could forget February 18!), I baked John's favorite cake and said it was a birthday cake for the dog. When baseball season starts, I plan to have a small gift (perhaps a baseball pen or pencil) at his place at the dinner table—wrapped, of course. (Maybe I'll even put the gift in multiple boxes. It is never too late to learn.) I am so glad that God will take all of our parenting and transform it into something very good if we love him and truly want his purposes.

TAKE INVENTORY

Jean Fleming (*A Mother's Heart* [Colorado Springs: Nav-press, 1996], 93–98) explains how we can take spiritual inven-tories of our children. She emphasizes being alone with God, thinking about and praying for our children, and then writing each child's strengths, weaknesses, our observations, and ap-plications. This is excellent advice.

I think it would be great for a mother to keep a spiral note-book for *each child* with the following sections: prayer re-quests/answered prayer, child's perceived strengths, child's per-ceived weaknesses, mom's personal observations, character traits that need to be developed, applications. (You may want to look to Scripture to see who in the Bible reminds you of your child.) Whether you have a toddler or a teenager, this would be beneficial, indeed!

Remember what we said earlier about moms in chapter 5: *Never think of yourself as "just a wife and mom." You're a molder of leaders, a gatekeeper of peace, a channel through which God's Word can be instilled into the next generation. Add to this list "teacher who understands the individual shape of her children."* As godly mothers we want to raise children who desire to please God and fulfill his plans for their individual lives. (And as a friend reminded me, God's plans may not be ours.)

Even Mary, Jesus' mother, had to learn about her son. In Luke 2:41–52 we are told of Jesus staying at the temple, unbeknownst to his parents.

> After three days they [Joseph and Mary] found him in the temple courts, sitting among the teachers, listening to them and asking them questions. Everyone who heard him was amazed at his understanding and his answers. When his parents saw him, they were astonished. His mother said to him, "Son, why have you treated us like this? Your father and I have been anxiously searching for you."
>
> "Why were you searching for me?" he asked. "Didn't you know I had to be in my Father's house?" But they did not understand what he was saying to them.
>
> Then he went down to Nazareth with them and was obedient to them. But his mother treasured all these things in her heart. And Jesus grew in wisdom and stature, and in favor with God and men. (vv. 46–52)

Had Mary been keeping a journal on Jesus' development, she probably would have observed that he independently went to the temple, and then he replied to their concerns that he had to be about his "Father's business (KJV)". Under application Mary may have written, "I will ponder this child God has given me, knowing that he is God incarnate, the Savior of the world."

Biblical Examples of Weaknesses

My family has to continually rely on the Lord in our weaknesses. I like to turn to Scripture and see how the Lord deals with real people with real weaknesses. Exodus 2:11–12 tells us, "One day, after Moses had grown up, he went out to where his own people were and watched them at their hard labor. He saw an Egyptian beating a Hebrew, one of his own people. Glancing this way and that and seeing no one, he killed the Egyptian and hid him in the sand."

Moses thought he was justified in killing the Egyptian. After all, he had been beating a Hebrew. But when Pharaoh heard about the murder, he tried to kill Moses (Exod. 2:15). That's why Moses fled to Midian, where he became a shepherd and learned humility and submission. When God came to Moses years later and said, "I am sending you to Pharaoh to bring my people the Israelites out of Egypt" (Exod. 3:10), he found a different Moses from the one who killed the Egyptian.

"But Moses said to God, 'Who am I, that I should go to Pharaoh and bring the Israelites out of Egypt?' And God said, 'I will be with you'" (Exod. 3:11–12).

Where was the overconfident Moses? The one who took it upon himself to kill an Egyptian? The one who would have said earlier, "Sure, I can do that myself"? Moses had been to school and he was ready to graduate and enter the arena of God's good purpose. Moses was looking to God and not to himself.

Who else showed us how to focus on the Lord and not ourselves? Well, we are told in Luke 8:1–2, "After this, Jesus traveled about from one town and village to another, proclaiming the good news of the kingdom of God. The Twelve were with him, and also some women who had been cured of evil spirits and diseases: Mary (called Magdalene) from whom seven demons had come out."

Mary Magdalene had been changed. We see in Matthew 27–28 how she later followed Christ through his crucifixion, death, and resurrection. The same Mary Magdalene who had been controlled by seven demons was a witness to the angel's proclamation that Christ had defeated death and had risen from the dead. I believe that God had prepared her to accept such a miracle. After all, she personally knew the miracle that Jesus Christ had wrought in her own life. She knew what it was like to be controlled by demons and what it was like to be controlled by the Lord. God had worked all things in Mary Magdalene's life for good, as she had been called to his purpose.

Mom, what child have you been entrusted with? What child has God given you for a few short years? Scripture tells us that our children have been "fearfully and wonderfully made" (Ps. 139:14). It's truly an awesome responsibility to parent a child—the hope of the next generation.

SCRIPTURES FOR REFLECTION

Train a child in the way he should go,
and when he is old he will not turn from it.

PROVERBS 22:6

Read and reflect on 1 Corinthians 1:27–31.

QUESTIONS TO PONDER

1. What are the unique "bents" (God-given temperament and traits) of my children? What are some of their strengths and weaknesses?

2. How can I train my children according to their bents?

3. Are weaknesses good or bad? Why or why not? (You may want to refer to Paul's words in 2 Corinthians 12:7–9: "To keep me from becoming conceited because of these surpassingly great revelations, there was given me a thorn in my flesh, a messenger of Satan, to torment me. Three times I pleaded with the Lord to take it away from me. But he said to me, 'My grace is sufficient for you, for my power is made perfect in weakness.' Therefore I will boast all the more gladly about my weaknesses, so that Christ's power may rest on me.")

4. What does God want me to do with my weaknesses? With my children's weaknesses?

5. Who in the Bible does my child resemble in character? How did God teach this person? (Example: Moses was self-reliant. After he spent years in the desert, he learned humility and submission and was ready to be used by God.)

CHAPTER 12

A WALK WITH THE WISE—
PART ONE

RITA, JANET, AND BETSY:
WORKING MOMS WHOSE
HEARTS ARE AT HOME

The whole secret of abundant living
can be summed up in this sentence:
"Not your responsibility but your response to God's ability."

CARL F. H. HENRY

Isn't it wonderful to encourage one another and share experiences as we journey through life! Scripture tells us in Proverbs 13:20, "He who walks with the wise grows wise." The book of Titus stresses the importance of older women teaching younger women: "Likewise, teach the older women to be reverent in the way they live . . . to teach what is good" (v. 2:3).

I benefited greatly from the counsel of another mom shortly after the premature birth of our first son Christopher. Phillis Lavender had delivered premature twins shortly before Chris was born. She personally knew the worries of a mom who wondered if her baby would live through the night. And she truly understood how it felt to love a son so much, and yet not be able to bring him home—to entrust him to the walls of a hospital rather than to the loving arms of parents. No one, not even my own mother, gave me so much hope as Phillis, for she had walked in my shoes—on the very paths where I was traveling.

Let us now look into the lives of several friends of mine who juggle family responsibilities with employment outside the home. Although their occupations vary—nurses, an attorney, secretary, manager, technician, and cardiac ultrasound technologist—each considers her God-given assignments to her family to be her primary calling. Their stories echo the lives of thousands of married and single moms who want to keep their hearts at home.

Rita's Story: *"My kids see me as a mother first."*

Mother

My Mother has blond hair about to her neck.
She is about five-foot three.
My Mother washes clothes,
washes dishes, mops, sweeps the kitchen,
cooks food, and bakes.
She is fun and nice, too.
My mom is a lawyer.
Kyle Looney

• • •

I love you mom,
You are the best.
But theres much more,
Listen to the rest.

You are nice,
You are kind
You read labels all the time,
You love dogs,
So do I,
And we both love nana's apple pie.

This poem was dedicated
to the best mom ever!
Becca Looney

Tears welled up in Rita's eyes when she shared the above Mother's Day cards written by her son, Kyle, and daughter, Becca. "My kids see me as a mother first," she said. In the jagged penmanship of little children, Kyle and Becca had honored their mom as a Proverbs 31 woman. They had called their mom blessed as they recognized her sacrifices for those she loves.

Rita has been practicing law for almost fifteen years. Despite this, she says, "I am a mom twenty-four hours a day. My priority is family. If I get a phone call from school, I am out the door."

Rita and her husband, Randy (who is also an attorney), discussed raising children even before they began practicing law. When Rita began interviewing with law firms, she told them up-front that she planned to work part-time when and if she had children. This was mutually agreed upon when she entered the legal profession.

After Rita had worked for almost three years, Becca Looney was born. Following an extended maternity leave, Rita returned to part-time work at the law firm that had initially hired her—just as she and Randy had planned. She worked four days a week from 9:30 A.M. to 2:30 P.M. These hours enabled Rita to have a calm morning with her family and ample time home in the afternoon to prepare dinner. I am reminded of the Proverbs 31 woman who watched over the affairs of her home and prepared for future needs. Before Becca was even conceived, Rita anticipated how she would adapt her work schedule for her family. When Rita accepted her first job as an attorney, she knew that she would be free to work part-time should the Lord bless Randy and her with children.

When asked what advice she would have for moms working outside the home, she replied, "A mother must first be concerned with the care that her kids will receive when she works." Rita says that she was fortunate, indeed, with child care arrangements. After being initially cared for by a wonderful Christian friend, Becca and Kyle were watched by their own grandmother (Randy's mom) while Rita worked outside the home.

Rita encourages mothers to look into the possibilities of part-time employment. She says, "There are part-time positions available for professionals. There is more and more flexibility today in the workplace with computers, cell phones, and faxes."

Today Rita works alongside her husband while the kids are in school. She drops them off at school and picks them up in the afternoon. Their afternoons are filled with music lessons, playing with the dog, going to the mall, and just having fun together.

I asked Rita if her professional life ever seems to overflow into the home. She admitted that this does occur at times; however, she constantly strives for balance. She recalled several years ago when she was involved in a lengthy trial, one that virtually claimed one month of her life. As a result of this, she evaluated her priorities and is no longer involved in litigation. Like you and me, Rita tries to continue doing what she does well and corrects areas where she falls short. She challenges herself to place her time before God, allowing him to examine her heart and motives.

Rita said that although Randy is a great help to her, "We're not a Mr. and Mrs. Mom. I'd say that Randy's main role is being the dad." Rita added that since Randy is self-employed, he often helps by picking something up for supper, bringing the children to and from school, or watching them if she should have a meeting after school hours.

Like most kids, Becca and Kyle have regular responsibilities at home—feeding the dog, helping with laundry, and doing chores. The Looneys have a chart on the refrigerator that gives values to various extra chores. When the children want to earn extra money, they know exactly what will be expected of them for particular sums (example: wash windows, 50 cents per window; vacuum stairs, 75 cents, etc.). They have various tasks to perform each week—twenty to be exact—and they are given an allowance of 10 cents per task. If they complete 100% of the tasks, they receive an extra $2 for excellence. Although Rita and Randy have utilized various charts and systems, Rita said their children are taught to be obedient to them as their parents, and not to a system.

When Rita travels from time to time, she prepares envelopes for Becca and Kyle—one for each day that she will be gone. The envelopes contain notes from her along with small treats such as gum or Sweet Tarts. She also likes to call home while the kids are in school so she can leave a message on the answering machine, telling them how much she loves them. And she tries to bring something home for the kids to let them know she was thinking of them.

Rita has had to cut back on some commitments in order to be sure that she is meeting the needs of her family. Although she believes it is important for a Christian to be involved, her prayer is that she would do what God wants her to and that she would be an effective wife and mom. And she believes that it is important to reevaluate commitments and work situations— at least annually. Rita said, "A decision that was right for a time may not necessarily be right forever."

Rita's mother taught her the importance of placing her husband before her children. Rita recalled the words of her mom right before she married Randy: "You will be tempted to let your children be your focus. But your husband must come first. Your father has always been first and I hope you never felt slighted." Rita said that she never did, and that her mom's faithfulness to her dad has been a great example for her.

Rita believes that husbands must support working wives. "If the husband does not want his wife working outside the home, then you must follow his lead," she said. "Be sure that your husband is first and that he does not get the leftovers."

So how does a professional woman juggle home and family? She continually seeks the Lord's will and places family before her profession. Nothing is sweeter to her ear than when her kids call out, "Mom, I love you! Will you make some cookies today?"

* * *

Janet's Story: *"Do not let Satan bring false guilt to you. If he knows home is your heart's desire, that is where he is going to try to get to you."*

Although more than twenty years have passed, Janet Greenwood still vividly remembers "the years of the locusts"—those when her children seemed to know day care more than mom care. She prays regularly that God will redeem the years that she lost with her son and daughter. But Janet cautions moms who must work for one reason or another, "Do not let Satan bring false guilt to you. If he knows home is your heart's desire, that is where he is going to try to get to you."

Trying to balance home and work responsibilities took its toll on the early years of the Greenwood family. While Janet was working full-time as a nurse, her young husband, David, was not only employed full-time, but also taking some college courses. Although they lived in the same house, they rarely saw each other. With two small children, the Greenwoods found themselves in the midst of a marital crisis. Although money was tight, Janet quit her job to restore her home.

Janet prayed fervently that the Lord would provide a flexible job which would allow her to be a godly wife and mother. When she was offered a weekend shift as a nurse (which still allowed time for her to attend church with her family), she felt that God had answered her prayer. Janet gratefully accepted the position and found that it enabled her to be involved with her family and with her children's school activities.

Like Rita, Janet has regularly evaluated her employment options outside the home. After working the weekend shift for more than a dozen years, she recently began working three twelve-hour shifts during the week. This better fits the needs of her family today.

When asked for advice to young women, Janet said:

- When considering various careers, anticipate how they will affect your family.
- If you want to stay home when you have a family, save *at least* half of your salary as a cushion for the years when you will stay at home with the kids.
- Be aware that your perspective and priorities can change once your child is born. Your job may not seem so important when your child cries each morning as you leave him at day care.
- When considering a job, see if there are any other working mothers there. If possible, ask them if the work environment is "family friendly."
- Establish friendships at work. You'll find that you will help one another out.

- Teenagers need you as much as little ones. You are physically exhausted with little ones, and emotionally exhausted (from praying for wisdom) with teenagers.

Janet's husband has been an active dad. He willingly changed diapers, coached basketball teams, and helped with the school car pool when needed. When Janet worked weekends, he prepared the Sunday meal. He also lowered his housekeeping standards, realizing that a working mom cannot do it all. Janet recalled with a smile how David once took care of the kids and the house when he was between jobs. After being with the kids for several days he said, "Now I know what you do all day." Nothing can beat firsthand experience, can it?

When I asked Janet how she handles housework, she replied, "Well, our house would not be condemned, but it is not spotless." David and the kids do pitch in and help, but housework at the Greenwoods is primarily Janet's responsibility. She has taught her children not only how to clean, but also how to do the laundry. "Part of my responsibility as a mom is to be sure that the kids will know how to take care of themselves," she said. She tries to focus on the big picture and what is truly important for her family.

Janet tries to exhibit a sensitivity to her husband. Since he does not like clutter on the desk in the kitchen, she makes an effort to keep it neat. He also appreciates a vacuumed house, and by making this a priority she shows that she cares about him.

When asked about parenting tips, Janet mentioned that it helps teens accept consequences when they are agreed upon and posted—prior to offenses. She gave me an example of this concerning driving:

For speeding: One day's driving privileges lost for every mile over the speed limit.

No seat belt: Removal of three days' driving privileges (if either the driver or passengers do not have on seat belts).

Passenger in the back of the truck: Removal of driving privileges for one month.

Janet has been very active in her church and with her children's schools, but she has had to learn to say no to some very good things. Before taking on extra responsibilities, she seeks the Lord's wisdom through prayer and gets input from her husband. He supported her desire to drive the kids' sports teams to games as she is able to be with her children and their friends and is privy to teenage conversation.

"Know your kids," suggests Janet. Because her oldest daughter Sarah really appreciates hugs, Janet has come up with creative ways to give her hugs while she is away at college. On Valentine's Day she stitched hearts on pillow cases for Sarah and her roommate, and on Sarah's pillowcase she lovingly sewed the word "Hugs." She has also made a quilt from Sarah's high school club and sport T-shirts. When Sarah uses it, she can't help but think of those who love her at home.

What would Janet have done differently? "I would not have worked full-time when the kids were little. I would not put myself in that situation. Those were some precious years; I missed seeing my daughter's first step, hearing her first word. I just did not realize then how precious those years were and how quickly kids grow up."

Finally, Janet wants to remind moms that God is sovereign, and that he, indeed, can redeem the "years of the locust."

* * *

Betsy's Story: *"Scripture tells Christians not to be unequally yoked. If you are a Christian and marry a non-Christian, your marriage will be in third gear—the core ingredient for a dynamic marriage, Jesus Christ, will be missing."*

Although Betsy's three daughters are now married to fine Christians, she recalls some stressful years in her marriage when her husband did not know Christ as Lord and Savior. Betsy met Tom when he was in law school and fell head over heels in love with him.

Shortly after their marriage, she realized that Tom did not have a personal relationship with Jesus Christ. Although he did believe in God, he saw no sense in the Bible, church, or Christian friends. Betsy knew then that her life with Tom would not be easy, but she was committed to her marriage vows.

With mounting bills, Betsy herself chose to return to work when the kids entered school. Coming home in the evenings to a dirty house and a myriad of chores caused her to feel defeated—especially if Tom mentioned that the house needed to be cleaned. However, through the years she has realized that Tom is very willing to help her with specific chores—he just needs to understand specifically what she wants him to do. She also understands that she needs to keep the emotion out of conversations when she is tired. She tries to simply answer Tom's questions, not to take them personally.

When Betsy first realized that Tom did not know the Lord, she thought that she could persuade him to become a Christian—that she could change him. But over time, and after much prayer, she now realizes that Tom's relationship with God is between God and Tom.

She still recalls seasons when she went to church alone and was very angry. Tom would take the girls to the lake and tell them that church was not important. One Sunday, Betsy became very frustrated and decided that she would put her foot down and prohibit the girls from going to the lake with their dad instead of going to church.

However, on that particular Lord's Day the sermon was on 1 Peter 3:1: "Wives, in the same way be submissive to your husbands so that, if any of them do not believe the word, they may be won over without words by the behavior of their wives." She was reminded through her pastor's message that she could accomplish more through prayer than by fighting with her husband. On that day, more than twenty-five years ago, she gave her husband and marriage over to God. But she kept praying.

Betsy vividly recalls a conversation she had with her oldest daughter, Pam, while they were together in the car. At the time Pam was dating a non-Christian.

"Mom, why would it matter if Joe is a non-Christian? After all, Dad's not a Christian," she said.

"Pam," Betsy confessed, "life with your dad has been like living in a divided house."

At that point, it was as though the Holy Spirit gave Betsy the seemingly perfect words to say.

"Pam, try to start the car in third gear," Betsy said.

She did so, and the car's engine began to strain.

"Your dad and I connect emotionally, physically, and intellectually, but we do not connect spiritually—we just don't have the power. Right now the car is moving, but not at its full capacity because we're in third gear. Dad's and my marriage is good; but because he's not a Christian, we don't have full power."

Betsy went on, "Pam, Scripture tells Christians not to be unequally yoked. If you are a Christian and marry a non-Christian, your marriage will be in third gear—the core ingredient for a dynamic marriage, Jesus Christ, will be missing."

Pam got the point.

Five years ago, Tom found himself in the midst of a crisis. His mother was dying and he could do nothing about it. Although he was used to controlling things, he could not control life and death. His own mother led him to the Lord as she explained to Tom that her incomprehensible sense of peace resulted from the fact that she absolutely knew that she would leave this world only to be in the presence of the Almighty God.

She opened her tattered Bible and shared the words of Romans 10:9, "If you confess with your mouth, 'Jesus is Lord,' and believe in your heart that God raised him from the dead, you will be saved." The Holy Spirit moved in Tom's life at that point. In front of his very own mother, he repented of his sins and prayed to receive Christ as his Lord and Savior. He wanted to have the same assurance of his eternal destiny as his mom. His wife's and mother's prayers, had finally been answered.

Tom now docks his boat on Sundays and goes to church with his wife. Betsy says that the last five years of their marriage have been their happiest ever.

If you are discouraged, think of Betsy. Remember: "All things are possible with God" (Mark 10:27).

SCRIPTURES FOR REFLECTION

Plans fail for lack of counsel,
but with many advisers they succeed.

PROVERBS 15:22

But Jehoshaphat also said to the king of Israel,
"First seek the counsel of the Lord."

1 KINGS 22:5

Do not be anxious about anything,
but in everything, by prayer and petition,
with thanksgiving, present your requests to God.

PHILIPPIANS 4:6

I can do all things through Him who strengthens me.

PHILIPPIANS 4:13 (NASB)

QUESTIONS TO PONDER

1. How did Rita and Randy plan for children?

2. What one suggestion from this chapter could help me this week?

3. How do I seek the Lord's will and place my family before my profession?

4. If you have any "years of the locust" that you would like God to redeem, describe them below and ask the Lord to give you wisdom and peace concerning these years.

5. What is the Lord saying to me through the stories of Rita, Janet, and Betsy?

CHAPTER 13

A WALK WITH THE WISE—
PART TWO

SUE AND CAREY:
WORKING MOMS WHOSE
HEARTS ARE AT HOME

A friend is one who comes in when the world goes out.

ANONYMOUS

You've just met Rita, Janet, and Betsy—three women—three stories—but one Lord loves them completely. Now, you will meet two more of my friends, Sue and Carey.* Both women know not only the bliss of married life, but also the agony of divorce. And both have witnessed firsthand the unsurpassing trustworthiness of God.

Sue's Story: *"I felt very small, weak, and incapable. I had to trust God."*

---

* Sue and Carey are fictitious names. Some details about their lives have been altered.

"I used to look at couples divorcing and say, 'How did they get where they are?'" Sue said those words prior to 1994—before she knew the pain of divorce. She had not seen it coming. How did it sneak up on her? Ralph returned from work one day and simply announced, "I am having an affair with another woman. I love her and want to marry her."

Sue was devastated. She felt rejected knowing that the man she loved wanted another more than he wanted her. She thought she had been a good wife and mother. How could Ralph have ignored his wedding vows and chosen another? But Ralph's mind was made up. There was nothing she could do. Or was there?

Sue's pastor had taught that when challenges hit, seek stable ground. She explained to me that if someone's car went over an embankment and landed in a swollen creek, they must first "seek stable ground" by keeping their mind alert and getting out of the car. If they did not, and panicked, they would be trapped in the car and would drown. Sue did not want to drown.

She recalled one of her pastor's sermons: "God always knows what you should do," he said. "Bring thoughts from tragedy back to God's Word."

"How will God help me through this?" she wondered. With two young children, she knew that she had to trust God. "I felt so very small, weak, and incapable. I had to trust God. I had to stand on my faith and his many promises," she said. Sue's story is one of God's faithfulness. As the Lord was with Moses and Joseph, he was with Sue. "Jesus Christ is the same yesterday and today and forever" (Heb. 13:8).

Ralph had told Sue that she and the kids could continue living in their home until the children graduated from high school. Sue began an in-home business and worked on crafts when the children were asleep. Initially it looked as though she would not have to enter the work force to provide financially for her family. But once again Ralph did not live up to his promises.

When he stopped paying his child support, Sue just could not make ends meet. But as God would have it, she found herself returning to work at the very time the church (that housed her children's school) needed a part-time secretary. God was, indeed, leading her, and she accepted this position.

Because Sue knew nothing about today's technology, the pastor's wife taught her how to use computers (a skill that would prove vital to her in the future). Sue thought she was beginning to get a hold on her new life. But not for long. Ralph stopped paying the house note, and Sue and the kids found themselves evicted from their home. Sue was back on her knees.

"God tells me in his Word that he loves and cares for me," she said. "I was not asking for a mansion. I knew he might provide a trailer. But I knew he would give the kids and me a roof over our heads."

Scripture continued to comfort and direct Sue in her struggles. She claimed Philippians 4:13: "I can do everything through him who gives me strength" and Romans 8:28: "In all things God works for the good of those who love him, who have been called according to his purpose." She totally trusted that God would lead and direct her, and she prayed fervently.

"God picked me up and comforted me. There were days when I literally prayed all day. The pain was so bad. I could not pray that God would lead me day by day. Rather, I had to pray that he would lead me moment by moment."

Two weeks before Sue and the children had to vacate their home, they were told about a missionary couple who were going overseas. They wanted someone to live in their house. Sue rented the missionaries' 1,800-square-foot home for only $200 a month. Once again God had tangibly shown Sue that he was leading the way. He had not forgotten her.

Ralph then stopped paying tuition for the children's Christian education, and he no longer provided medical insurance for them. Sue's seemingly ideal job as a church secretary was not to be long-lived. She knew she would have to seek employment where she could get some needed benefits for her family. She was told about a position at a Christian ministry where she was hired as a full-time secretary. It was clear to her that her prior training at the church had been invaluable—computer experience was a requirement for her new position.

Sue continued to look to the Lord and he remained faithful. When she needed understanding ears, friends were there for her. "When I had to mow the yard myself," she said, "my mother and sister were there to help me. When I needed child care after school and during the summer months, friends volunteered to care for the kids—they would not accept any money."

Today, it seems as though Sue's tale has had an almost fairy-tale ending. She has remarried a wonderful Christian man and says that she has forgiven Ralph and feels no bitterness toward him. Her children love their new dad and accept him totally. Her son even wrote his new dad the following letter:

Dear Dad,

During Bible class today our teacher read us part of 1 Corinthians 13. Then she asked us who we thought of. It didn't take me long to think of you. You are long suffering and kind. You are not proud. You do not behave yourself unseemingly. You are not easily provoked. You are not happy when someone is hurt. Your life is not filled with glamour and money. You will not be remembered by the world after your death; but the people whose lives you have touched will always love and remember you.

Indeed, God had provided not only for Sue but also for her children!

Today Sue continues to work at the Christian ministry in order to pay for her children's Christian education. However, once again, God has provided. She is now in a position that allows her to work from 8 A.M. to 3:20 P.M. Tuesday through Friday. And she is off in the summers!

Sue does have some good advice for working mothers: "There may be things in your life that you enjoy (such as art work or painting) that you will have to put aside for a season so you can interact more with your children. But, for example, if you love gardening and can get your kids to enjoy gardening, then you can have the best of both worlds."

Sue realizes that God helped her so that she can help others. As we are told in 2 Corinthians 1:3–4, "Praise be to the God and Father of our Lord Jesus Christ, the Father of compassion and the God of all comfort, who comforts us in all our troubles, so that we can comfort those in any trouble with the comfort we ourselves have received from God."

In the midst of the juggling act, in the midst of discouragement, in the midst of divorce—is God faithful? Ask Sue.

* * *

Carey's Story: *"Be as organized as possible because it is impossible to have it all."*

If you had driven by the attractive two-story suburban home of Dr. and Mrs. Bob Jackson, you would probably have noticed their perfectly manicured lawn, beautiful rose garden, and sparkling BMW. If you happened to have driven by a little before 8 A.M. you may have caught a glimpse of a smartly dressed woman loading her daughter and two sons into the family van for the short drive to Frederick Heights Christian Academy. After Carey dropped the kids by school, she went to the local hospital where she worked four hours a day. She was grateful for her schedule because she had plenty of time to run errands before she picked the children up from school.

Carey and Bob appeared to have it all. They were both well respected in their professional circles, active at church, in the community, and in their kids' schools. But this changed on April 1, 1990—the day Bob told Carey that he had been having an affair with one of his nurses. Enraged, wounded, hurt— words are inadequate to express the myriad of thoughts and feelings that reverberated through Carey on that day. How could she have not seen this coming? It was as though a Mack truck had plowed into her head-on; but the wreckage was not metal—it was her family.

Bob and Carey had been members of Second Baptist Church for fourteen years, so they turned there for pastoral counseling. They both knew that God says in Malachi 2:16, "I hate divorce." And they both wanted to recapture the love they once knew—for themselves and for the sake of their kids. After an initial separation of two months, Bob returned home to Carey and the children. But the nightmare wasn't over—the cycle began again, and again, and again. After three years filled with reconciliation, affairs, and several separations, Carey finally had enough. She filed for divorce.

At that point, Carey found herself feeling confused. "This was not the picture I had of my life," she said. "I had been so hurt." But as Carey turned to the Lord and sought godly counsel, she saw the Lord open doors for her and lead the way in a dark time. She lived the truth of 2 Samuel 22:29: "You are my lamp, O LORD; the LORD turns my darkness into light."

After her divorce, Carey tried to keep life as consistent as possible for the children. Although Carey exchanged her part-time job for the full-time hours of a cardiac ultrasound technologist, the children continued to attend Frederick Heights Christian Academy. When the academy's tuition became financially impossible, she and the children moved to a nearby community where the children were enrolled in public schools.

And Carey found herself with a forty-five-minute commute to work.

Today Carey rises at 5 A.M. so she can prepare her family's breakfast, lunch, and dinner for the day. Before departing for work, she writes notes for the children that communicate her expectations and also encourage them. Since she does not want them to ever feel like they are all alone or abandoned while she works, she carries a pager and cellular phone. She wants the kids to be able to reach her and to know that she is available to them at any time. She is also generally home in the evening, able to eat dinner and share the day's happenings with those she loves.

Life has really changed for the Jacksons over the years. Carey has dropped out of her bridge club, church choir, and no longer teaches Sunday school. She said that there will be plenty of time for her to do these things when the kids are grown. She has had to reduce some of her expectations and decide which areas of the house she wants to keep presentable. She just doesn't worry about the rest. She has also learned to choose her battles and focus on her relationship with her children.

Carey recalled one day when she literally fell on her face with tears in her eyes, asking the Lord for his hand of direction. At that very time she received a phone call inviting her to join a group of moms who pray regularly for their children's schools and teachers. Carey joined the group and it has been a source of great encouragement for her. Since she did not want to leave her children more than absolutely necessary, the group now meets weekly at her home.

For those who find themselves in Carey's situation, she has several suggestions for you: "Be as organized as possible because it is impossible to have it all. You also need to let friends and people who love you minister to you. I am a giving person and it was hard for me to do this, but it has been so wonderful."

She also said, "I would really make sure there is a godly man who will mentor your sons. I was hesitant to ask for this. Boys need to see how a godly man acts who loves his wife and loves his kids. I wish I had actively sought someone to mentor my boys."

"Through all of this," she says, "I have learned how good God is and how he has totally and completely taken care of me in every aspect of my life even though I have bucked some, because I sure did want to be a stay-at-home mom."

SCRIPTURES FOR REFLECTION

For where your treasure is,
there your heart will be also.

MATTHEW 6:21

Praise be to the Lord,
to God our Savior, who daily bears our burdens.

PSALM 68:19

You are awesome, O God in your sanctuary;
the God of Israel gives power and strength to his people.

PSALM 68:35

But you, O God, do see trouble and grief . . . ;
you are the helper of the fatherless.

PSALM 10:14

QUESTIONS TO PONDER

1. How do I tangibly show my family that my heart truly is at home?

2. (If married, answer these questions, and then discuss them with your spouse.)
   - What are some specific ways that I work with my spouse for the good of our family?

   - What are two strengths of my marriage?

   - What are two areas where my spouse and I need to grow in our marriage?

   (For a single mom)
   - What are two specific ways that I have accepted the help of others?

   - In what area do I need to enlist help?

3. When did God tangibly show his faithfulness to me?

4. Meditate on the words of Hebrews 13:8: "Jesus Christ is the same yesterday and today and forever." What is God saying to me today?

5. (For married moms) What child do I know from a divorced home who needs my help? What is one way that I can reach out to this child?

6. (For single moms) Who could I ask to be a godly mentor for my child?

CHAPTER 14

A WALK WITH THE WISE— PART THREE

LAURA AND MAURY: WORKING MOMS WHOSE HEARTS ARE AT HOME

*We know not what the future holds,
but we do know who holds the future.*

WILLIS J. RAY

In this chapter we'll visit with two more working moms: Laura Martin, who juggles her roles of pastor's wife, mother of two, and full-time employee; and Maury Quo, who has cut back her hours at work to be home with her new daughter, Emma.

Laura's Story: *"Use every opportunity you get to teach spiritual values and educational facts to your child."*

God gives every believer different gifts, and Laura believes that he has given her a gift of administration. (As you read her story, you will probably agree.) She is grateful for her time management skills because they have enabled her to keep the right priorities while maintaining her focus on her family. Laura loves people and thrives on activity. She was named Mrs. Arkansas in 1996, and from time to time she speaks at churches and judges various pageants.

Kenneth and Laura have been married for almost a decade and have two sons: Matthew, 7 years, and Seth, 4 years. Kenneth works bi-vocationally as a pastor, and in three short years his congregation has grown from fifty active members to more than three hundred. Although Laura sings in the church choir and is very involved in her husband's church, she also works forty hours a week as a manager of customer service representatives for a Christian ministry. How does she do so much?

First, she and Kenneth prayerfully consider priorities for their family. They often pray together and fast when bringing matters before the Lord. When Laura wanted to return to the work force two years ago, she knew God wanted her main focus to be on her family. That's why she was upfront during the interview process—letting it be known that she needed a job with flexibility. Laura explained to her future supervisor her desire to continue as a field trip mom and PTA board member.

As a result, today she works from 6:30 A.M. to 3:30 P.M., and is free to take her lunch hours or vacation time to meet the needs of her family. During the Christmas holidays Laura takes time off from work to be with her family, and she is able to work fewer hours in the summertime.

Laura's parents are very involved with Matthew and Seth. Being retired, they love to have the boys spend the night when there are school holidays. When the boys visit their grandparents, Laura separates clothes for each day, pinning notes indicating which clothes are for which day. She also gives grandparents needed schoolbooks and homework assignments.

Laura writes everything down on paper and tries to maximize her time. Routine is very important to her. A typical day at the Martin family would look like this:

- After preparing for work herself, Laura gets bowls and spoons out for her family. She also begins one load of wash. She leaves for work, which begins at 6:30 A.M.
- Kenneth supervises the boys' dressing for school. (Laura lays out their clothes the night before, actually placing them in a bookcase. One shelf is Matthew's and the other is Seth's. She lays the boys' clothes out in the order that they will put them on—from the shirt on top to the shoes on the bottom.)
- Kenneth drops the boys off at school in the mornings. (Laura places the boys' backpacks in Kenneth's vehicle the night before—complete with signed notes, needed money, etc.)
- Laura and Kenneth meet for lunch every day at their home. Laura removes the clothes from the washing machine and places them in the dryer. She also runs the vacuum if needed. Then she and Kenneth discuss things at lunch and often pray over family matters.
- Laura picks up the boys from school. She takes them to Tae kwon do on Tuesdays and Thursdays, and Kenneth picks them up. (Laura keeps clean Tae kwon do uniforms in the back of her car.)
- Laura folds clothes and prepares dinner (Wednesday is pizza night!). After dinner, Kenneth bathes the boys (except on Wednesdays—Laura is in charge of baths then).
- Fridays are family nights. The boys generally choose activities to do with their mom and dad—eating pizza, a favorite videotape, etc.

Laura said that she could not balance work and family responsibilities without the help of her family. Kenneth, Laura, and the boys are a team. She often can be found typing Kenneth's notes for church, and the boys will collate them. The boys also help her make gift bags for older members of the church and special treats for church members on various holidays. And Kenneth often takes the boys to church with him to give her some special time to herself.

Laura encourages working moms, "Use every opportunity you get to teach spiritual values and educational facts to your child." Because the Martins' church is about sixty miles from their home, they find themselves spending a lot of time in the car. They have found that this travel time provides a great opportunity for family conversation. Laura also likes to help the boys read various signs while they are in the car, and she gives Matthew and Seth activity sheets for the car.

Laura really appreciates the flexibility of her job. She is grateful that her work schedule allows her to be very involved in her boys' school, and she has found, "If you will take interest in your children, you'll find that the teachers will take an interest in them, too." Laura's job has enabled her to grow, not only professionally, but also spiritually. She continually prays that the Lord will help her be discerning and spiritually perceptive as she meets the needs of her family and employer.

When asked if she would have done anything differently when it comes to work and family, Laura said that she would prefer to work only three days a week. But then she added that she believes she gets more done when she is working.

Laura believes that her real strength comes from Jesus Christ. She said that the most important things anyone can have are: a personal relationship with Jesus Christ, time studying the Word, and fellowship with believers. As it says in Psalm 119:105: "Your word is a lamp to my feet and a light for my path."

Yes, God's Word will illuminate the paths of working moms like Laura, you, and me. But in order for our paths to be illuminated, we must regularly turn on the lamp.

* * *

Maury's Story: *There were six couples and six babies—soon to become six families through the miracle of adoption.*

If you have ever talked with someone like Maury Quo, the words of Ephesians 1:5 likely took on new meaning for you: "He predestined us to be adopted as his sons through Jesus Christ, in accordance with his pleasure and will."

As Christians, you and I are adopted into the family of God. After I visited with Maury, I gleaned a bit of the joy that must fill the heart of our Lord as he looks upon his own adopted sons and daughters.

Maury and Geoff Quo had longed for a child of their own. After being married for six years, they were truly overjoyed when they learned that they would be blessed with a little girl. But she would be no ordinary daughter. Although the Quos lived in Arkansas, little Emma was thousands of miles away in China.

The day Maury and Geoff first saw their child is forever etched in their hearts. There were six couples and six babies— soon to become six families through the miracle of adoption. Maury explained that each couple had traveled to the same hotel in China to receive their babies. A phone call announced "The babies are coming." Words cannot describe the incomprehensible sense of excitement and wonder that filled the Quos' hearts. They were truly in the midst of a labor of love.

The hotel's elevator opened and the scurrying of footsteps could be heard coming down the hall. Finally, after all the years, the Quos were presented with the gift they had so longed for. A child. A little girl—their legacy. Life would never be the same.

After spending several days in China, and traveling for forty-one hours back to the United States, Maury and Geoff brought their new daughter home. Maury still has to pinch herself today when she sees little Emma. Every day she thanks God for her, realizing that Emma is truly a miracle. Maury said that she and Geoff must look uncommonly excited as they take their new addition out into the community. She questions if other new parents feel the same wonder and awe that they do. "We must appear like newlyweds. I'm sure some question why we are so excited. But we've just waited so long!" Maury said.

Although the Quos had discussed Maury reducing her hours at work when she became a mother, they had been concerned about the financial impact this would have on their family. After all, they had depended on two paychecks for years. But the day they saw Emma, Geoff said, "Maury, why would you want anyone else to care for such a precious child?"

So, after much prayer and a three-month leave from work, the Lord seemed to clearly answer Geoff and Maury's prayer for direction. Maury received a phone call from the hospital where she had been employed asking if she would consider working one day a week as a CAT (computerized axial tomography) technician, and be on call every five to six weeks. Maury thought, *What could be more perfect?* and accepted the position.

She is grateful for the opportunity God has given her to stay at home with Emma, while keeping her skills sharpened at work. Yes, Geoff and Maury have had to make some sacrifices. Today they rarely eat out, and Maury even has to watch the food budget at the grocery story. And the new car they had planned to purchase—why, it's just a dream.

Maury is grateful for her work schedule. She enjoys the camaraderie that she continues to share with fellow employees and relishes the opportunity to run errands one day a week during her lunch hour. But she also feels that her extra hours at home have resulted in a more relaxed environment—one that has provided her with extra energy for her growing family. Maury describes herself as a "neat freak," and her limited work schedule enables her to not only keep the house in order but, more importantly, to really get to know little Emma.

Maury's advice to working moms: "Our society almost demands that we women make something of ourselves besides wives and mothers—as though being wives and mothers is not enough. If you want to be at home with your family, do not be tempted by the world to change your priorities and motivations."

After visiting with Maury, I was reminded of the following poem:

> Not flesh of my flesh,
>
> Nor bone of my bone,
>
> But still miraculously my own.
>
> Never forget for a single minute
>
> You were not born under my heart, but in it.

ANONYMOUS

(Jayne E. Schooler, *The Whole Life Adoption Book*
[Colorado Springs: Pinon Press, 1993], 13)

SCRIPTURES FOR REFLECTION

Like arrows in the hands of a warrior are sons born in one's youth.
Blessed is the man whose quiver is full of them.

PSALM 127:4–5

If any of you lacks wisdom, he should ask God,
who gives generously to all without finding fault,
and it will be given to him.

JAMES 1:5

Trust in the Lord with all your heart
and lean not on your own understanding;

in all your ways acknowledge him,
and he will make your paths straight.

PROVERBS 3:5–6

But the fruit of the Spirit is love, joy, peace, patience,
kindness, goodness, faithfulness, gentleness and self-control.

GALATIANS 5:22

QUESTIONS TO PONDER

1. What are five character traits that I want to model and teach my children? (You may want to refer to Galatians 5:22.)

2. How am I modeling and teaching these traits to my children?

3. What is the Lord saying to me concerning how I am modeling and/or teaching these traits to my children?

4. What five adjectives describe my home? (Examples: loving, peaceful, busy, cluttered, Christian, tense, hectic, calm, etc.)

5. What five adjectives does my child use when describing our home?

6. What five adjectives would I like to think of as describing my home?

7. What is the Lord saying to me about my home's environment?

CHAPTER 15

THE ONE WITH THE POWER TO KEEP OUR HEARTS AT HOME

I have a great need for Christ;
I have a great Christ for my need.

C. H. SPURGEON

It's hard to believe that our journey together will soon end. But before it does, we will chat about what I think are the two most important topics in this book: *Who has the power to keep our hearts at home,* and *Where do we go from here?*

Throughout this book, we've looked at how we can keep the right priorities—God first, then our families, and finally our jobs. As I began writing this chapter I prayed that God would somehow guide my hand so that I would write exactly what you need today.

Ephesians 6:6 reminds us of the importance of "doing the will of God from your heart." I find it interesting that the heart desire of someone far greater than you or me—Jesus Christ—was to do the will of his father. Jesus said in Matthew 26:39b, "My Father, if it is possible, may this cup be taken from me. Yet not as I will, but as you will."

It's hard to comprehend the tremendous love that our Lord has for us. Why would Jesus Christ have given up his place at the right hand of the Father in heaven to come to a comparatively insignificant planet called Earth and die on a cross? It just doesn't make common sense, does it?

Hopefully, the following illustration may help you. Recently some electrical cables shorted out, resulting in an underground fire and the loss of electrical power for about forty-two blocks of the downtown area of my hometown—Little Rock, Arkansas.

"'A chunk of concrete the size of a videocassette recorder apparently caused the blackout that darkened downtown Little Rock late Saturday and early Sunday,' officials said. 'The 1 1/2 foot-long, 1-foot-wide and four-inch-thick piece of concrete fell from the rim of a manhole and struck the low-voltage wires below. . . . It was a freak thing. . . . In this particular case, it hit such a perfect area—one that wasn't protected by fuses—so the fire didn't go out'" (*Arkansas Democrat Gazette,* March 10, 1998, 1B).

How could a piece of concrete the size of a VCR strike an unprotected place and darken literally blocks of the city? I sure did not understand this, but I am glad the experts did. Although they had to cut electricity to fight the underground fire, power was restored when the fire was extinguished.

Picture it. Darkness—even the most technologically advanced computers could not operate without power.

The point is this: I once was in spiritual darkness. Oh, I was a good person—probably tried to be too good. I definitely wanted to please other people and thought if I could do enough good works, then maybe I could get to heaven one day. I imagined some sort of massive scale in heaven. Saint Peter would put my good works on one side and my bad works on the other side. I would watch nervously to see which side would tip the scale. How I hoped it would be the good works!

Hoping for eternity. Trying—and yet falling short time and time again. It was so frustrating. I had a void within me and knew that I could never be good enough to merit eternal life. I definitely believed that Jesus Christ died on the cross for sins, but I did not believe that he died for *my* sins. I thought I had to work my way to heaven. It was as though someone had a wonderful present for me that I was trying to earn. Yet in reality, I could only receive it when I willingly accepted it as a free gift.

I was like someone in a darkened area of Little Rock who refused to turn on the lights after the power had been restored. Why wouldn't I "flip the switch"? Because I did not understand the power that was available. I did not have the faith. And so I continued in darkness.

Thankfully, through friends and Campus Crusade for Christ, the Holy Spirit turned on the light and opened my eyes to the truth found in Scripture:

> Brothers, my heart's desire and prayer to God for the Israelites is that they may be saved. For I can testify about them that they are zealous for God, but their zeal is not based on knowledge. Since they did not know the righteousness that comes from God and sought to establish their own, they did not submit to God's righteousness. Christ is the end of the law so that there may be righteousness for everyone who believes. . . .
>
> That if you confess with your mouth, "Jesus is Lord," and believe in your heart that God raised him from the dead, you will be saved. For it is with your heart that you believe and are justified, and it is with your mouth that you confess and are saved. As the Scripture says,

"Anyone who trusts in him will never be put to shame."
(Rom. 10:1–4, 9–11)

I had finally found the secret. I realized that I could *never* be good enough to merit eternal life—only a perfect God could pay for the sin against a holy Creator. I admitted that I was a sinner who could not earn her way to heaven, and I said a prayer accepting Jesus Christ as my personal Lord and Savior. At that point I had new life and an eternal destination (1 Pet. 1:23). Just as the light was restored to a dark downtown area, so too did light flood my life. The void in me was gone forever.

I remember asking myself, "Why would the God of the universe become man and willingly allow himself to die on a cross? Why wouldn't he have chosen another way for salvation—an easier, less painful way?"

We cannot understand the mind of God. We cannot comprehend his unmatchable splendor and holiness. Isaiah 55:8–9 tells us, "'For my thoughts are not your thoughts, neither are your ways my ways,' declares the LORD. 'As the heavens are higher than the earth, so are my ways higher than your ways and my thoughts than your thoughts.'" Even Moses was told in Exodus 33:20, "You cannot see my face, for no one may see me and live."

Holiness. There are few examples of holiness today. No wonder it is hard for many to believe by faith that Jesus Christ died on the cross for their sins. Only the death of the perfect God-man could pay the penalty of sin. And to think that he willingly died on a cross for Adam's sin, for Eve's sin, for yours, and mine.

Romans 6:23 explains that the wages of sin is death. Even when I tried to lead a sinless life, I just could not do it. That's why I was so thrilled when I learned that by putting my trust in a perfect Savior, Jesus Christ, then my sins were forgiven forever.

What would have happened in Little Rock if the power switches were not turned on—even after the problem had been isolated and the raging fire had been extinguished? The people would have remained in darkness when they could have so easily chosen the light.

John tells us that Jesus Christ is "the Lamb of God, who takes away the sin of the world" (John 1:29b). And Jesus himself said in John 8:12, "I am the light of the world. Whoever follows me will never walk in darkness, but will have the light of life."

Mom, Jesus offers you and me the gift of eternal life. He has extinguished the penalty of sin once and for all. His power is available to you and to me, but he does not force us to turn on the switch. We have to do it ourselves.

Perhaps you are a Christian, but still struggle with sin in your life. I think you will be ministered to by the following paragraphs that tell how we can replace our "me" mentalities with a desire to please Christ day by day. I first read this in a Great Hills Retreat Ministry flyer entitled, "Not I, but Christ":

> The following are some of the features and manifestations of the self-life. The Holy Spirit alone can interpret and apply this to your individual case. As you read, examine yourself in the very presence of God. Are you ever conscious of:
>
> A secret pride; an exalted feeling, in view of your success or position; because of your good training or appearance; because of your natural gifts and abilities. An important, independent spirit?
>
> Love of human praise; a secret fondness to be noticed; love of supremacy, drawing attention to self in conversation; a swelling out of self when you have had a free time in speaking or praying?
>
> The stirrings of anger or impatience, which, worst of all, you call nervousness or holy indignation; a touchy,

sensitive spirit; a disposition to resent and retaliate when disapproved of or contradicted; a desire to throw sharp, heated flings at another?

Self-will; a stubborn, unteachable spirit; an arguing, talkative spirit; harsh, sarcastic expressions; an unyielding, headstrong disposition; a driving, commanding spirit; a disposition to criticize and pick flaws when set aside unnoticed; a peevish, fretful spirit; a disposition that loves to be coaxed and humored?

Carnal fear; a man-fearing spirit; a shirking from reproach and duty; reasoning around your cross; a shrinking from doing your whole duty by those of wealth or position; a fearfulness that someone will offend and drive some prominent person away; a compromising spirit?

A jealous disposition; a secret spirit of envy shut up in your heart; an unpleasant sensation in view of the great prosperity and success of another; a disposition to speak faults and failings, rather than the gifts and virtues of those more talented and appreciated than yourself?

A dishonest, deceitful disposition; the evading and covering of the truth; the covering up of your real faults; leaving a better impression of yourself than is strictly true; false humility; exaggeration; straining the truth?

Unbelief; a spirit of discouragement in times of pressure and opposition; lack of quietness and confidence in God; lack of faith and trust in God; a disposition to worry and complain in the midst of pain, poverty, or at the dispensations of Divine Providence; an overanxious feeling whether everything will come out all right?

Formality and deadness; lack of concern for lost souls; dryness and indifference; lack of power with God?

Selfishness; love of ease; love of money?

These are some of the traits which generally indicate a carnal heart. By prayer, hold your heart open to the searchlight of God, until you see the groundwork thereof. "Search me, O God, and know my thoughts: and see if there be any wicked way in me" (Psalm 139:23, 24 KJV). The Holy Ghost will enable you, by confession and faith, to bring your "self-life" to the death. Do not patch over, but go to the bottom. It alone will pay.

> Oh, to be saved from myself, dear Lord,
> Oh, to be lost in Thee;
> Oh, that it might be no more I,
> But Christ that lives in me.

AUTHOR UNKNOWN

> *"Create in me a clean heart,*
> *O God; and renew a right spirit within me"*

PSALM 51:10 (KJV)

Mom, my prayer for you today is that you know Jesus Christ as your personal Lord and Savior and call upon him to empower you in your juggling act as a working mom. Jesus Christ is the only one who can truly keep our hearts at home—giving us the power to focus on our Lord and families.

SCRIPTURES FOR REFLECTION

> *Jesus said, "You are from below; I am from above.*
> *You are of this world; I am not of this world.*
> *I told you that you would die in your sins;*
> *if you do not believe that I am the one I claim to be,*
> *you will indeed die in your sins."*

JOHN 8:23–24

*And this is the testimony! God has given us eternal life,
and this life is in his Son. He who has the Son has life;
he who does not have the Son of God does not have life.*

1 JOHN 5:11–12

QUESTIONS TO PONDER

1. Do I believe that I will go to heaven? Why or why not?

2. How do the Scriptures tell us that we can be confident of an eternity with the Lord?

3. (Reread the paragraphs from the Great Hill Retreat Ministry entitled, "Not I, but Christ.") In what areas has the Lord convicted me of sin?

4. What action points do I need to take in light of my answer in question 3?

5. Would I describe myself as a proud or humble person? How does this match up with the character of Jesus Christ?

6. How can I share my faith in Jesus Christ with others?

7. How can Jesus Christ help me balance my home and work responsibilities?

CHAPTER 16

WHERE DO I GO FROM HERE?

Little drops of water
Little grains of sand,
Make the mighty ocean
And the pleasant land.

Thus the little minutes
Humble though they be,
Make the mighty ages
Of eternity.

JULIA A. FLETCHER

Several weeks ago my husband, Jim, and I were helping in a special needs Sunday school class at church. Most of the students are young adults who are developmentally delayed. The teacher was explaining to the class that God loves us forever.

When she asked, "Do you know how long is forever?" a woman in her twenties started swinging her arms through the air and laughing aloud. With the innocence of an eight-year-old, she responded: "Yes, yes, I know how long is forever. It's one year."

This sweet student is not capable of even beginning to understand the concept of forever. Nor am I.

"One year"—as the words flowed from her lips, I knew in my own heart that she had said something quite profound that touched me deeply. It was as if I had a picture of how God must depict my efforts at trying to understand his ways.

I am reminded of Psalm 103:15–16:

> *As for man, his days are like grass,*
> *he flourishes like a flower of the field;*
> *the wind blows over it and it is gone,*
> *and its place remembers it no more.*

If I were to live my life as though its length were only one year, how would I live it? Do I really picture the seeming trials of this world in light of eternity? Since I can't comprehend eternity, then do I picture my life with a view of spending thousands and thousands of years in heaven?

More than twenty years ago, as Jim and I would drive together to work, we would see an older man laboring in his massive garden. He didn't know that his diligence was being observed by at least one young couple. As the days were transformed into months, and the months into years, so too did his garden change. It seemed to grow smaller in size and finally was just a bed of weeds. Then one day we noticed a For Sale sign in front of the house. I never knew the man who lived in the house, but somehow his garden reminded me of life. I imagined that he grew too old to continue its upkeep, and then one day he passed from this earth to eternity.

As I ponder the years remaining in my life, where does God want me to go from here? Does he want me to make any changes? Is he pleased with how I am using the talents he has given me?

God has spoken to my own heart as I have written *My Heart's at Home*. And as I evaluate my current role in life, I challenge you to do likewise.

What does God value? What do you and I value? Ephesians 2:10 tells us, "For we are God's workmanship, created in Christ Jesus to do good works, which God prepared in advance for us to do." May we be so in tune with the Lord that we recognize his divine hand of guidance. May we realize how God orchestrates our lives and prepares good works for us to do.

No matter what lies ahead in future years, I want to follow the advice of Christian author Margaret Jenson. She said that her mother told her to always choose a humble and thankful heart—even when she did not get her way. As working moms, we too must have thankful hearts. We must make the most of the time that we do have with our families and look to tomorrow with a cheerful and expectant attitude.

Proverbs 27:19 says, "As water reflects a face, so a man's heart reflects the man." Mom, may your heart and mine reflect women who truly love the Lord . . . women who love their families. Ones whose hearts are at home.

SCRIPTURES FOR REFLECTION

Trust in the Lord with all your heart
and lean not on your own understanding;
in all your ways acknowledge him,
and he will make your paths straight.

PROVERBS 3:5–6

Delight yourself in the Lord
and he will give you the desires of your heart.

PSALM 37:4

Humble yourselves, therefore, under God's mighty hand,
that he may lift you up in due time.
Cast all your anxiety on him because he cares for you.

1 PETER 5:6

QUESTIONS TO PONDER

1. Complete the following chart:

What does God value?	*What do I value?*
Where does God want my focus?	*Where is my focus?*
What does God promise in Proverbs 3:5–6?	*Do I need to make any changes?*

2. What does the Scripture say about anxiety (see 1 Pet. 5:6)?

3. How do I exhibit trust in God despite circumstances?

4. How does my life reflect a person whose heart is at home?

more great resources for you and
your home

Because credit lines and loans have become a way of life, the children of today have been enticed by companies promising instant gratification – buy now, play later! Mattel has even come out with "Cool Shopping Barbie" – this female role model comes complete with Mastercard and checkout counter. There is a corporate conspiracy to entice the youngest of children into believing that there is an urgency to buy now! We as parents owe it to our children to raise them to realize the value of the dollar, spend cautiously, and save. *This is one book you can't afford to be without!*

0-8054-1518-1   *Debt Proof Your Kids*

AVAILABLE AT FINE BOOKSTORES EVERYWHERE

more great resources for you and
your home

Julia Childs and the Galloping Gourmet – stand back, Mimi Wilson and Mary Beth Lagerborg are showing today's cooks how to spend more time *out* of the kitchen! Enormously helpful and completely practical, *Once-a-Month Cooking* offers complete plans for cooking an entire month's (or two weeks') dinner entrees in just one day! Resolve to cook less but enjoy mealtimes more in the new year!

0-8054-1835-0   *Once-a-Month Cooking*